THE FACES OF JUSTICE

THE FACES OF
JUSTICE

SYBILLE BEDFORD

faber and faber

This edition first published in 2011
by Faber and Faber Ltd
Bloomsbury House, 74–77 Great Russell Street
London WC1B 3DA

A CIP record for this book is available from the British Library

ISBN 978–0–571–28268–5

To
Janet Flanner

We see the Judges move like lions, but
we do not see what moves them.

JOHN SELDEN

Good laws lead to the making of better
ones ; bad ones bring about worse. As
soon as any man says of the affairs of the
state, " What does it matter to me ? " the
state may be given up for lost.

JEAN JACQUES ROUSSEAU

" Write that down," the king said to the
jury, and the jury eagerly wrote down all
three dates on their slates, and then added
them up, and reduced the answer to
shillings and pence.

LEWIS CARROLL

CONTENTS

PART ONE

ENGLAND

I

An Ordinary Trial

Above the dais, the ornate chair, the robe, the still head of the Judge rises above the court as if suspended.

"Thirty-two cheeses, my Lord, valued three hundred pounds four shillings and nine pence."

The first moments inside a Court of Law are like the first moments at a play—the eye notes the scene, sound begins to reach the ear, then words. Sense converges later.

The Judge's head does not stir. It is the head of a man aged first into a face only, the face of a very old woman, aged now into a fine dry shell, the almost transparent covering of precise slow workings—an ear, a brain, a hand. For, at some distance, animated by the same mechanism, there is a hand, a hand moving, a hand with a pen, moving, writing, writing on, in a steady small compass.

"My Lord, we will establish to the satisfaction of the members of the jury——" Resonant and deliberate, it is the Crown : a massive Treasury Counsel, florid, bursting with self-possession, speaking up-right from the well of the court, rocking himself to and fro in front of the advocates' bench.

"With respect——" Another gowned figure has leapt to his feet. "My learned friend is perfectly aware that the cheeses were never found."

"I would invite your Lordship's attention to Count Two, Count Two of the Indictment."

England

" The apples ? " The voice of the Judge is disincarnate ; but audible enough to those in practice.

" I respectfully submit that the apples have been traced."

" *Res ipsa loquitur ?* "

" Quite so, my Lord."

The jury shift a little. Twice six persons, three of them women, fitted to two benches, one above the other, in an open box that seems just to hold them. They also seem much alike, grey, absent-faced, thin-suited people : civilians firmly stuck to their place in this scene of adorned, articulate and accomplished men.

" You may put in the apples, Mr. Maule," says the Judge. There is now a trace of urbanity in the voice.

" Thank you, my Lord."

The other figure subsides. Someone hands him a screw of paper. He glances at it and tosses it over his shoulder to a junior on the bench behind. The junior, a fine sheep's face under a square-fringed wig of dirty white, pushes up his spectacles to read, then passes on the paper further down the bench. Another junior taps counsel on the back ; two string-bag wigs meet in confabulatory hisses, black cloth billows.

The Crown has resumed ; the Judge's hand is moving.

The pit, the few square feet of centre floor free of pews and boxes, is filled with two large tables, stained biscuit-brown like all the other boarding, a-flutter with a snowstorm of documents. Here solicitors and their clerks labour in pin-stripe or blue serge and their own hair, passing charts and schedules like cruets at a lodging house. The Clerk of the Court, in a stall of his own below the dais, sits toga'd behind a stack of foolscap, looking at his fingernails, suddenly seizes a telephone one has not perceived before and hardly trusts is there, cups his hands over his elegant theological face and the instrument, and is seen speaking into it but not heard.

An usher moves about softly, careful not to trip. A handful of extraneous and upset looking people sit neatly in the three more short rows of bench squeezed by the entrance door.

An Ordinary Trial

A tall Silk, splendid as Pompey, strolls into court, bends over a colleague who turns up a dimpled Boswellian face, whispers loudly, flings himself into a seat, crosses his fine legs, shoots out an arm in a robust yawn ; then picks himself up and walks out again.

At the far end of the court, in the largest box of all, on an axis with the Judge's chair, sits the prisoner in the dock. It is a neat, close-knit, youngish man, and he too holds himself very still. He sits on his chair in the front of that capacious loose-box, very much alone, the second cardinal point in the cat's-cradle of all the eyes, the thoughts, the emotions. His small, smooth face is all profile ; smarmed palish hair, pale stretched baby-skin, showing the bones, showing the skull, showing the thoughts move : swimming slowly, carefully, showing the nerves stretch ; showing fear. He has the look of the not so young man who did not wish to grow old, the look of the shifty man-servant. . . . And all of the time he is face to face with the head and the hand that are the Judge.

In the dock with him like an idle umpire in the ring, sits a warder in uniform, bulky, relaxed, unconcerned.

The charge is fraudulent conversion to his own use and benefit of certain property. He is, in fact, accused of having stolen some apples and some cheeses from his employer.

The time of day is about eleven o'clock of a winter morning ; the place is Number Two Court—or was it Number Four ?—of the Central Criminal Court in London. The Old Bailey.

That case, or one like it—it was a very ordinary case—came on some four or five years ago. *Mutatis mutandis*, it could come on this year and it could come on, God willing and if this particular judge has not retired, next year and the year thereafter. I walked in on it by chance when I was first trying to learn the ways of our law courts. I have sat since through many cases of all kinds, but that one was the first criminal trial and the paragraphs above, with a few enlargements, are what I wrote of what I saw at the time. Now, I propose to go through this case—in memory as well as words in black on white—with a fine toothcomb. For I have decided to start on a journey to the law courts of some other countries, and I want a kind of yard-stick. Before going off to see how they are doing it elsewhere, I want to put down, if I can, commit to mind and paper, the look, the sound, the ways of some daily English trials.

We had missed the beginning. The gradual filling of the place with men and papers; the Judge's coming on with the flurry of sudden rising and subsiding which is the stroke of trans-substantiation into Court. The popping-up, immediately afterwards, of the prisoner, shot from the floor into a box. The calling of the jury, one by one, name by name; their oaths; the ordered opening moves gone through with detachment and dispatch; the formal charge read by the clerk; the plea (" Not Guilty ") before counsel was able to get up and begin, " May it please your Lordship ", and outline the prosecution case.

The facts appeared to point in one direction. They nearly always do until one's heard another side. On the Fourteenth Day of December last (in counsel's words) Crawford, the accused, a van-driver by occupation was instructed by his employer's office to pick up a consignment at a certain warehouse and deliver it to Messrs Mawlesbury, Fruiterers & Provision Merchants in the Borough of Kensington. Cheeses and apples—six barrels of Coxes—were put into his van; cheeses and apples were seen driven off; no cheeses and apples arrived at Messrs Mawlesbury's. Shortly afterwards, the accused left his job. He could not be found at the address he had left. When he was arrested, he had on him the receipt for a £200 deposit on a motor-car. Apples, an undomestic amount of them, were found in the dwelling house of the accused's brother-in-law ; apples had been offered for sale to a coster-monger on the Fulham Road by a man answering the accused's description.

One-pointed, if not flawless. " I am calling Mr. Hobson," says counsel.

The usher makes for the door. Mr. Hobson, who has been hanging about outside, comes in, charges his way into the varnished pulpit, stumbles on the step, rights himself, grasps the Bible held out to him and repeats, " I swear to Almighty God——"

" I swear *by* Almighty God," says the usher.

" By Almighty God——That the evidence I shall give—— Shall be the truth," says the witness, his mind quite evidently on the correct order of words and his own voice.

" Your name," says counsel, " is Daniel Reginald Hobson, and you reside at one hundred and eleven Elm's Road, Kilburn ? "

" That's right, sir."

" And your occupation ? "

" Stock clerk."

" You are at present employed by Messrs Mawlesbury ? "

" And have been for fifteen years, sir."

" Will you describe for us the nature of your activities ? "

" I check what comes in."

" Will you tell this court what took place on the 14th of December last ? "

" I was saying to Miss Gusnip in the morning—she's the cash register—I hope, I said——"

" Never *mind* what you were saying."

" You must confine yourself to direct statement of fact," says the Judge. He does not say it at all unkindly.

" I was hoping that Trundle & Carter's was not letting us down again——"

" I'm afraid we can't have that, Mr Hobson," says counsel.

" Forget about Trundle & Carter," says the Judge.

Between them they manage to give acceptable shape to what did not happen on the 14th of December last. " What was your construction, Mr. Hobson ? " said counsel.

" Pardon, sir ? "

" How did you account for the missing consignment ? "

" Muddle."

" Muddle ? "

" Seeing the season, sir."

The Judge shows desire to be enlightened.

" Christmas, your Honour."

" Very well."

" So you did nothing to trace the apples and cheeses at the time ? " says counsel.

" Not till the bills came in January."

" Invoices for this particular lot which you were positive never came to hand ? "

" Positive."

Counsel bows. " That concludes the evidence of this witness, my Lord." But the defence is waiting.

" Mr. Hobson——" It is the man with the charming, clever, eighteenth-century face who had smiled on Pompey. " Mr. Hobson, Christmastide is a very *busy time* in your line of work? "

" Yes, sir."

" A time when hundreds, if not thousands of pounds of oranges and bananas and nuts and dates and er—pineapples would be passing through your stores ? "

" Oh, yes, sir."

" And *barrels of apples*? Yet you pretend that in all that hullabaloo—if I may use that expression—you remember *not* having received one particular small consignment ? "

" I never saw no T.&C.'s six barrels of Coxes."

The Defence desists and sits down.

Other witnesses are called. A warehouse porter ; a garage hand ; a police inspector ; an office clerk. Scrap by scrap, the Crown tries to establish every one of the facts alleged.

An Ordinary Trial

Ours is the accusatorial system, and here it is at work: you have seen fit to bring a charge, it is up to you to prove it. The accused—although he may have waited for his trial in prison—is considered innocent in the eyes of the law from the moment his trial begins. From witnesses, prodded into narrow track by question upon patient question, from bills and ledgers, it becomes evident beyond sensible doubt that there was a van, that this man and no other drove it on that day, that this man was alone, that cheese and apples existed in the material space and quantity and time. The court—a handful of men who spend their adult years training for and practising this kind of discipline—advanced by taking two steps backwards; what could be held an obvious, a transparent case of guilt, is assembled, as if the straws of every brick were shining new, before the judge who must have heard it all a thousand times, the blank-faced jury, and in sniping range of the defence. The law that must seem to hound, also protects the silent prisoner in the dock; the formidable wheel stays its course, standing still almost before it may crush this exceedingly small fly.

The costermonger is in the box now; he has been made to put his story together. Counsel is coming to the climax, he is off-hand, affable.

" And is the man who offered you these cheeses anywhere in this court ? "

" Yes."

" Can you point him out ? "

The witness does not lift his hand. " In the dock," he says in a low voice. He does not look at the prisoner.

" Have you any doubt ? "

" No doubt, sir."

" Your witness, Mr. Clare."

Defence counsel rises deliberately. " Mr.——Willoughby, you told my learned friend that you turned down those apples." He, too, is affable. " Why ? "

" The price wasn't roight."

" The price wasn't right." Then very quickly, " What was wrong with the price ? "

" He asked too little."

" How much ? "

" I can't say I remember, sir."

" Come, come, man, you are telling his Lordship and the members of the jury that you refused to buy because the price was not right, and yet you cannot remember the price ! "

" It didn't seem right at the time, sir."

" Mr. Willoughby—fruit is a fluctuating commodity ? "

No answer.

" The price of fruit varies ? "

" It may do."

" A great deal ? "

" Quite a lot."

" Quite a lot." Pause. "What is the right price for Coxes ? "

" Well, it all depends, sir——"

" Exactly." Cold and clear : " I suggest that you turned down these apples because you were afraid. You are not above snapping up a good thing, Willoughby, when it comes your way ? Are you ? I suggest you had not been, shall we say, overscrupulous about the origin of some of your wares and you thought you might be watched ? "

From anyone else, in any other place, such words could not have been spoken without consequence ; but counsel in court cross-examining as to credit, is privileged. Which means that if counsel thinks that he can discredit a witness's evidence by making the witness look a nitwit, a liar or a crook, he may try to do so. Sometimes the judge will cut him short, sometimes the attempt will back-fire, but the witness himself has no means to ward it off—except perhaps by his own honesty or intelligence—and for counsel there is no risk of libel, the forensic baiting has no reality outside. The witness often does not know this ; anyway to him it is all substantial as the cloth is to the bull, and Mr. Willoughby looks very sullen.

An Ordinary Trial

The jury's faces still reflect no opinion whatsoever.

The other side has one more word. There's nothing as unruffling as a brief smooth re-examination. " Mr. Willoughby," says Crown Counsel, " will you make it quite clear why you refused these apples ? "

Vehemently : " They looked fishy."

" Quite. And would you mind telling his Lordship where you habitually obtain your supplies ? "

" Well, there's the Devon Co-op, and from I.M.B. quite a bit . . . and the Ambulatory Vendors' Mutual."

" Thank you," counsel sits down, smugly.

Next comes a fragment of confident, packaged evidence from a police officer. " When I charged the accused with the offence, the accused said, ' Oh, it's about those cheeses. I know nothing about them. I don't know what happened to those cheeses.' "

This concludes the case for the prosecution. The defence calls the prisoner. And when at last he, too, stands in the witness-box, he seems weary of it all. He has pleaded Not Guilty and he is going to stick to it, but without much spirit or much hope. His story is that he went where he was told, accepted what was shoved into the van, drove off to where he was directed, day in day out from nine to five, and did not pay much notice. Defence counsel does what he can for him : Yes, he answers, he might have taken a load to a wrong address ; yes, it might happen ; no, he does not remember ; yes, someone might have hung on to the stuff ; yes, certainly. . . .

" Crawford——" it is the prosecution's turn to put the questions, " do you remember unloading thirty-two Gloucestershire cheeses at *any* address ? "

" I don't, sir."

" It was a large order, was it not ? "

" Not particularly."

" I suggest it was an *unusually large* order. What happened to those thirty-two cheeses ? "

" I must have took them where they was supposed to go—if they was in the van."

" To Messrs. Mawlesbury's ? "

" If that was the address."

" Perhaps I can refresh your memory. Mr. Dimdore, can we have Exhibit 9 ? Thank you. I see from the entries that you made deliveries at Mawlesbury's on December 11th—on December 4th, 3rd—on November 27th, 22nd, 15th, 9th. Is that so, Crawford ? "

" If it says so in the book it ought to be correct."

" It says so in your book, Crawford. The day book you kept and which we have here. Would you say that the entries in that book were correct ? "

" By and large."

" What do you mean ? "

" Just a manner of speaking."

" Crawford, on December 14th—the day the goods were due at Mawlesbury's—there is no entry in your book. The page for that day is a blank. Was that also correct *By* and *Large*, Crawford ? "

" I don't know."

" *Why was your book for that day a blank ?* "

The jury seem to have come out of their collective day-dream ; looks are fastened on counsel with something like avidity.

" Because I didn't fill it in."

" Why not ? "

" We often don't."

" Who are We ? "

" The other chaps."

Counsel rustles his notes. Then starts on a new track. The offer made to Willoughby, the costermonger.

" I offered him no apples," says the prisoner.

" You heard the witness identify you ? "

" I don't remember our conversation, I may have talked prices to him. . . ."

" For what purpose ? "
" I was thinking about setting up in business for myself."
" Business in apples ? "
" Yes."
" *And cheese?* "
No answer.
" Mr. Willoughby told us that you brought him a sample of Coxes ? "
" They were my own."
" They were your own ! Where did you get them from ? "
" A shop."
" Which shop ? "
" I can't remember."

" Crawford : I understand that you are a relatively poor man. You live on your wages. On December 19th—a few days after you took French leave from your job—you made a down payment in cash for a Vauxhall motor-car ? "
" I made a handsome income."
" Nine pounds a week ? "
" Well, a good income."
" Good enough to pay a cash deposit of two hundred pounds ? "
" I had savings."
" Where ? "
" In my savings' bank."
" May we have its name ? "
No answer.
" May we have the name of your bank ? "
" I kept it in the sugar-basin."
" In five-pound notes, no doubt."

" My Lord. Members of the jury——" We have reached the closing stage, the three concluding speeches. The Prosecution Case : a repetition of nearly everything that had been heard, hammered into a sober pattern, a common-sensical, an inevitable linking of effect to cause—it happened, it had to happen in exactly this way. " ' Oh, it's about those cheeses. I know nothing about them. I don't know what happened about those cheeses.' You will recall, members of the jury, the accused's words to Detective-Sergeant Brill when the sergeant was about to arrest him. Were these not the words of a guilty man? The words of a man who knows that the game is up and that his crimes have found him out——?" The Case for the Defence: " Members of the jury, as men and women of the world——" Memory is fallible, behaviour unaccountable, actions not always what they appear to be ; look at that loose end, take this one. " ' Oh, it's about those cheeses, *I* know nothing about them.' Could it not well have been that what the defendant was saying to Sergeant Brill was in effect, ' Oh, I am quite aware that there was a complaint about a load of cheeses that got lost during the Christmas rush, I am not a bit surprised that inquiries are being made about them, but the fact is that *I don't know* what happened to those cheeses.' Are these not frank words, members of the jury? The words of a man who has nothing to hide? You may well think, ladies and gentlemen, that the defendant made a muddle of his deliveries, you may think that he did not give due attention to his job, that he was negligent—but members of the jury, negligence and fraudulent conversion are poles apart ! You do not sit here to pronounce on the defendant's competence. You do not sit here to determine what ultimately became of the thirty-two Gloucestershire cheeses. *You sit to answer one limited question :* Has the prosecution satisfied you beyond reasonable doubt that Crawford dishonestly converted those apples and those cheeses ? "

When the Judge begins to speak there is great silence. The lawyers in the well have tied their briefs and settle back, arms folded in their sleeves. The jury look at the Judge, and never cease to look at him. He speaks for one hour and forty-five minutes and every fact and word are here again in a new order, and during the whole time one is gripped by a sense of watching the perfect automaton at work, the computer inside the old-fashioned illusionist's contraption in the cabinet of wonders—the Chess-Player, the Magician, hung with ermine and scarlet, deliver a creaking train of marshalled fact and datum, now from this angle, now from that, now tilted a fraction towards the middle, the Third Case, the Whole Case, the Synthesis of every case : You may well come to the conclusion that this is the one construction to infer, or you may think that it is not, but if you are satisfied in your mind that this is the right inference then you must say so and if on the other hand you entertain doubt as to that deduction then you must conclude that it is not safe to do so. . . .

Yet the issue, one feels, was decided when the prisoner stepped down from the witness box.

While the jury is out, the court begins the hearing of another case. Time, here, is not grudged ; nor is it wasted. The case, a bankruptcy offence of some intricacy, is between an ex-broker, four lawyers and the Judge. " Mr. Phillips has a large practice, dealing with the more unfortunate financial fortunes——" The well pays no attention. After forty minutes word comes that the jury have got a verdict. When they file back, everything moves fast. The foreman is standing, the man in the dock stands up too, then thinking he's made a mistake sits down again. The warder, who suddenly is no longer by the ringside but at his elbow, quickly gets him up again. The foreman has already said Guilty. One does not like to look at the prisoner now, and yet one does. In the last hour, the court has filled with broad-built men in serge with close hair-cuts and dispatch cases. They are police officers. The moment of truth has come. It is sordid. They step briskly into the box, efficiently repeat the oath and reel off the prisoner's record.

" There are five previous convictions, my Lord. On the 15th day of July 1953 sentenced at Manchester Assizes to twenty months imprisonment for larceny and fraud. On the 9th day of October 1951 by London Sessions for embezzlement . . .

" In August 1948 by the Swindon Magistrates for taking a watch from an employer . . .

" In 1947, for unlawful traffic in clothing coupons . . .

" 1939 by the Juvenile Court for taking and driving away a motor vehicle. . . ."

" He's a married man, my Lord, with three children, he served as a gunner during the war and was discharged with an excellent character."

" My Lord ! " The pretence is off, Counsel is no longer speaking for the jury, he is pleading for mercy with the Judge. It is still our learned friend with the dimpled face. " My Lord ! There are things we do that do not look well in the morning in the light of a court of law . . . No man is wholly bad—the prisoner's war record—early hardship—bad company —a patch of poor health—his present age : at a turning point—Another chance. I have here a letter from his sister."

The letter is passed up to the Judge who reads it inscrutably. Then he is ready. The clerk stands up and addresses the dock in monotone, ". . . You stand convicted of fraudulent conversion, do you know of any reason why this court shall not pass sentence upon you ? "

The prisoner stands wordless.

The Judge looks across at the prisoner.

" Victor Albert Crawford—what do you expect me to do with you ? " There is a pause. " You have made a proper mess of your life." Another pause. " I have no choice but to send you to prison again for a long time." The prisoner makes his first gesture. " Thirty months." The prisoner opens his mouth but the warder without quite laying hands on him has him away from the rail and into the back of the dock and down the trapdoor, he has vanished, it is over.

II

Summary Justice

Fifty thousand people a year, roughly, are accused of some offence or crime but less than a fifth of them qualify for trial at one of the higher courts. The panoply of Assizes and Old Bailey, the still leisured pace of Quarter Sessions, are only for the few; the rest are dealt with summarily by the magistrates. The magistrates, professional and lay, dispense instantaneous justice every working morning of the year. Summary, in half the cases, means dispatch from charge to sentence in one breath. People are brought into the dock still steaming with their deeds. Not here, the well-rounded lawyers' contest, the fine-culled point, the slanted pleadings—these courts are in the market place.

Put your hand in a pocket, strike a blow, snatch the orange; smile at the stranger, curse the cabby, cry your odds, and the law has swooped and has you by the scruff and in you go before the bench with your shopping bag, your load of beer, your evening clothes. . . .

" This is number one, sir, Patrick O'Connor."

" Patrick O'Connor you are charged with being drunk in the street do you plead guilty or not guilty ? "

"——guilty."

" This was at ten forty-five p.m. yesterday, your Worship in the North Elms Road."

" Any trouble ? "

" No trouble."

" Pay ten shillings."

" This way. *This* way."

" This is number two, sir, Joseph Andrew White."

Quick as small-arms fire. Burst cracks on burst from floor to bench to box, from box to bench to dock.

" At 11 p.m. last night, your Worship, outside the Crown & Feathers. He was lying on the pavement."

This came from the police constable standing in the witness-box. A young man, in uniform ; without the helmet of course. One can see the short new haircut.

The magistrate sits in the high chair behind his desk. His linen is as fresh as morning.

" Gave any trouble ? "

" *No* trouble, sir."

The magistrate very slightly alters his voice, " What do you want to say about this, Mr. White ? "

Something less than a sound comes from the dock. The defendant looks like what used to be called a respectable working-man, thin-faced, middle-aged, thin-lipped, grey. He is wearing a mackintosh.

" Do you want to *say* anything about it ? " re-enforces the gaoler who stands clip-board in hand at the mouth of the dock.

" I'm sorry for the inconvenience caused."

" Anything known ? " asks the magistrate.

" Nothing known, sir," the gaoler calls from the floor.

" Very well. Pay ten shillings."

" Ten shillings——! " someone takes up in the corridors.

The defendant now relaxes and looks ready to settle down.

" *This way*." The gaoler extracts him from the dock by sheer volition, manœuvres him across the floor and out of the door, at the other side of which the next man is held in reserve.

" This is number three, sir." The gaoler is a burly man in

uniform with a brush moustache and a thick pencil behind his ear.

The new accused is almost ludicrously disreputable. Blue chin, black eye, hair on end, a jagged hole in his coat where a sleeve ought to have been, filthy hands. This introduces a note of low comedy which, habitual though it must be in this place, is felt as slightly painful and to be ignored.

The clerk looks up sideways from his pen and paper and says his piece. " Alfred Davis, you are charged with being drunk in the street do you plead guilty or not guilty ? " It all comes in one gulp.

" Guilty, sir."

Another police constable briskly takes a step into the box and reels off time and place.

" Had any trouble ? " says the magistrate.

" He was singing and waving his arms."

" That was all ? "

" He was attracting a crowd, your Worship."

" I expect the crowd enjoyed it." The magistrate takes off his spectacles. " What do you want to tell us about this, Mr. Davis ? "

Speech, here, comes easily to everyone except the person in the dock. First he grunts, then he shrugs. " I wasn't feeling too well—I had a pint or two. . . ."

" Well, you know, Mr. Davis, it's a mistake to drink when you are ill." To the gaoler, " Anything known ? "

" On the 17th of January last, ten shillings for being drunk in this court."

The magistrate says, nose in ledger, " D'you admit the previous conviction ? "

" That's right."

" Fine of ten shillings."

" May I have time to pay, your Honour ? "

The magistrate looks up. " No."

" THIS WAY."

England

Number four is a woman. She is holding a basket. Her hair is dyed unevenly.

" There are five previous convictions for drunkenness, your Worship, two at Bow Street and three in this court."

" When did you say was the last one ? " asks the magistrate.

" 1956, sir."

" Well, you haven't been here for some years. Pay ten shillings."

" Ten shillings——" from outside.

The next man isn't sure what he wants to plead. He can't remember anything about it. Very well, then he must plead Not Guilty, says the magistrate. But when he is told to sit down and listen to the evidence, he changes his mind ; the plea is altered. Then up steps a seaman. The charge is drunk *and* disorderly.

" Any money on him ? "

It transpires that he has drunk his pay. What is he going to do now, the magistrate wants to know. Going back to sea next month. How does he propose to live until next month ? With the parents, in the North. The magistrate says he sees, but what about the fare ?

" I understand he has a married sister in court," says a police officer.

Number seven asks for time.

" Working ? "

" He's been out of work since the 19th of last month, your Worship."

" Fixed address ? "

" No fixed abode, sir."

" I don't know why all these people should come here to get drunk." The magistrate looks about the court. " This is getting the most drunken neighbourhood in London and I will not tolerate it. Ten shillings, Mr. Mills, or five days."

The defendant gathers himself to express surprised objection, but the gaoler is too much for him—here, too, no-one may stay on one split second after sentence has been passed—bristling with protest he is willed to step down and go.

Then it is the turn of two people, a man and a woman. They stand side by side behind the bar as the clerk arraigns them.

"Madeleine Z and Peter Y, you are charged with behaviour reasonably likely to outrage public decency."

The interiors of the dozen of London magistrates' courts vary slightly in size, arrangements and proportions. Like all law courts they are fitted to the last inch with the necessary amount of carpentry : benches, desks and stalls, biscuit-brown, disposed below the dais in some close but idiosyncratic pattern ; the docks, however, must all have been ordered from the same firm the same number of years ago. These fixtures are nothing like the ample wooden kiosks that fill so solidly the centres of the upper courts, here they are narrow, rectangular enclosures, raised a few steps above the floor and fenced on three sides by a narrow breast-high railing. A bench runs the length of these pens, and on the open fourth side, the gaoler keeps his guard. A single man or woman in the dock, however down-at-heel, however pugnacious, miserable or slick, is a human being alone, an individual isolated, in trouble. Two, crammed into that contraption, are at once reduced to an exhibit—on their feet, side by side, behind the grille they are for all the world to look at Box and Cox at bay.

". . . . at a quarter past midnight, your Worship, in a parked motor-car——"

"Yes ?"

The police witness tells the court. Briefly, and exactly.

"Anything you wish to say about it ?"

The man makes a gesture but stays silent.

"Of good character ?"

"Nothing about the man, sir. The woman's a known prostitute."

England

" Three pounds," says the magistrate in a colourless voice.
To the woman, " Fifty shillings."

All of this has reeled by as fast as print. The dove-tailed
entrances and exits, the sustained antiphonal flow, the quick
probe from the chair, the hint of cadenza, the conclusive
click—ten cases, a dozen cases, twenty cases put up, put
through their paces, judged and gone, and it is hardly more
than a quarter of an hour since court had opened. Each man
at his post on his toes, and each man with what he must
contribute on his file, his ledger, his notebook, on his clip-
board, on the tip of his tongue, and all the time the man in the
chair must have his hand on the reins and his mind on every
word, on every move, on every point. He is also usually
engaged in writing.

" Number twenty-one, sir," with a will, " All-ci-biades
Dī-onīdes."
A respectable-looking man is charged with receiving. " Do
you wish to be tried in this court," the clerk asks him as
fast as words will come, " or do you wish to be tried before a
judge and jury ? but if you elect to be tried in this court and
the magistrate finds you guilty of the charge and finds you
merit punishment greater than it is in his power to give he
can still send you to be sentenced at the other court, which do
you elect ? "
The man looks a bit at a loss, but says " Here," and
pleads guilty. The constable is already in the witness-box.
" Yesterday a.m., sir, on information received his shop was
searched——"
The magistrate cuts in. " Does he understand English ? "
" Oh yes, he does, your Worship." Very well then. Some
wireless equipment known to be stolen has been found.
" The accused admitted having bought it off a sixteen year
old boy. When charged with the offence the accused said,
' I believed the stuff was o.k. . . .' " And in almost the

32

same breath, " He's a married man, sir, with four children, he's been in this country since 1936, no previous convictions."

" Mr. Dionides," says the magistrate, " you realise this was a very silly thing to do——? " The tone is not unfriendly, rational.

" Boys dey come to the shop all de time wit tings to sell——"

" Don't interrupt the learned bench," three voices say at once.

" It is never wise to expect to get something for nothing, or to pay thirty shillings," the magistrate picks up the neatly-made flat box that has been handed up to him, " for something that must be worth at least twelve guineas." Increasing his pace, " Better not let it happen again. A fine of ten pounds."

" Thank you, sir." The defendant, expanding with relief, stumbles down.

Next comes a stray young man who does not appear to listen. He is accused of stealing forty-eight books of matches from a motor-car. " When charged with the offence, the accused said, ' I saw a piece of cake on the back seat of the car and I ate it. I was hungry.' "

" What does he do for a living ? "

" He says he works as a kitchen porter when he can."

" He'd better have a talk with the probation officer. Mr. Harper : can you see him this morning ? " Mr. Harper, who has been in court most of the time, half rises from his stall behind the press-box and says certainly. The magistrate makes his clear voice a little clearer, " I want you to have a talk with the probation officer who will be trying to help you." Kelly returns a listless glance and is prodded to give way to a deflated-looking man who has lost his tie.

" You are charged with being drunk while in charge of a motor-vehicle you are further charged with wilful obstruction of the police by resisting arrest and with causing wilful damage to a pillow, Metropolitan Police property worth fifteen shillings."

The defendant is asked whether he wants an adjournment to see a solicitor, and he decides he does.

" Sixty pounds," says the magistrate after what must have been a lightning calculation, for bail has to be both large enough and not prohibitive. It need not be put down in cash.

He is bustled over into the witness-box. Clerk : " And have you a sum of sixty pounds in money or goods after your just debts are paid ? " The tieless man swears he has. " Very well, remanded for two weeks on bail of sixty pounds on his own recognizance," says the magistrate. (But before the defendant is actually free to leave the building there will be a short delay while the police in some quick way of their own check up.)

Next there is an elderly woman, just looking plainly unhappy.

".... she stood by the counter for several minutes," this time it is a store detective who is speaking from the witness-box, a young woman, well put together. " I continued my observation and I saw her pick up a red plastic hand-bag worth one pound eighteen shillings and nine-pence and slip it under her coat. She then proceeded to walk towards the exit. I followed her. . . ."

The woman says, " I've never done anything like this before." She is scarcely audible.

" No previous convictions," says the police officer.

The magistrate speaks kindly. He is going to discharge her conditionally for twelve months. " You understand what this means, madam ? " If nothing like this happens in the next twelve months, " that will be the end of it, you won't hear about it again. But if there is a new charge, you can be brought here again and be punished for this charge. Do you understand that ? Very well. . . ."

A thick-set, youngish man with spectacles and a ready-made business suit, breathes through his mouth as he hears the charge which is taking and driving away a motor-car without the owner's consent. It turns out that he was just pushing the car along, round the square at two o'clock in the morning. It was after a party, he says. He never started the engine.

" A senseless action," says the magistrate and goes on to flay him.

With it goes the offence of driving a car without third-party insurance. This is automatic in all such cases ; you may think yourself insured to drive any car, but it is not so. There is always a clause : no owner's consent, no cover. The magistrate inquires about the young man's earnings. " Nine pounds five a week, sir, as an office clerk." The sentence is ten pounds plus forty shillings cost.

Next, a police detective clanks down a collection of iron-mongery in the witness-box. A young workman, rather aloof, stands in the dock. We have a hand-saw found in the prisoner's coat, a jemmy in his trouser-leg, a huge bunch of keys.

" Due to his rough appearance, I followed him. Questioned, the prisoner said, ' Oh, I just carry them round.' " There is also a pair of leather gloves. " ' My mother got those for me.' "

This constitutes unlawful possession of house-breaking instruments by night. Indeed, it can be an offence to go about with gloves in the dark hours if there's no lawful reason, such, one supposes, as the weather or one's ordinary standard of dressing.

The police wish to make further inquiries. " I respectfully ask for a remand of eight days," says the detective and gets it.

" Any objection to bail ? "

" There *is* objection, your Worship."

The magistrate hesitates. At this point it is up to him, within the lines of course laid down by Parliament, to grant or refuse bail. Bail is a statutory right. If bail is refused there must be reason, which is often simply reason to believe that one's man will not turn up again.

" He has no fixed employment or address, sir." The police

obviously are not keen on bail; if someone skips, it's up to them to catch him. "We also have grounds for thinking that another man may be involved."

"Very well," says the magistrate, "remanded in custody. 16th of April." Eight days is the longest a man may be remanded *in custody* before trial or committal for trial; but he can be, and is, remanded over and over again. If on the eighth day the court is booked up or if the police—or the defence solicitor—find they need more time, another remand is ordered.

The prisoner walks off, resigned.

Bail of course is a fundamental right, inherent in our presumption of pre-trial innocence. We all know, or ought to, what a week in custody may do to a man (on a charge, quite possibly, dissolving into acquittal or a fine). The magistrate must decide then and there on the facts apparent or supplied, and what may be an inconvenience to a tramp may turn into catastrophe for a bank clerk.

Another youth. The charge: stealing petrol from the tank of a motor-car.

"Not Guilty," says the youth.

The magistrate glances at the clock. "Then sit down and listen to the evidence."

This plea has turned the hearing into a trial. Everything will have to be *proved*. Proved from scratch to the magistrate —who now is judge and jury—by sworn and tested evidence just as it is done in the higher courts. As the defendant happens not to be represented, there are no lawyers in this case and the triangle here is between the magistrate, the youth and a senior police officer who now takes the floor to conduct the prosecution.

". . . . and are you the owner of an Austin saloon car, index number Q E D O O O ?"

And on the night in question was it parked in such and such a road? And had the witness gauged the petrol in the tank? He had. And how much was there? Six gallons. And later on was he invited by the police to inspect his car ? What did he find ? Two gallons in the tank—four missing. Thank you, says the inspector. The witness turns to go.

" Just a moment please," says the clerk. " Are there any questions you wish to ask the witness ? "

The youth has a peaked and pasty face but is otherwise rather well turned-out. His mouth opens a little, the gaoler jerks up a palm signing him to stand up. " I didn't go near your car," he says.

The witness looks at the chair.

" A *question*," says the magistrate.

The youth has now got his voice up to protesting pitch. " I didn't go near his car."

" You are an adult, you must know the difference between a statement and a question," says the magistrate. " You will be able to tell your side of the story when your turn comes. *Do* you want to ask the witness any questions ? "

The youth has subsided ; he shuffles and says, no.

This was his chance to test some of the evidence against him by cross-examination. But of course he hasn't the ability, nor the self-possession nor the knowledge, and who would at his age and in his place. He doesn't know about procedure, about what to expect and what to say *when*. (Surely, a few simply worded printed directions, given to him and the likes of him outside, would help ?) He might have asked the witness why he was so certain that he had that quantity of petrol in his car. When did he fill the tank ? Did he make a note about it ? How much driving had he done since then ? One could hear it all : " And is it not a fact, Mr. Smith, that you did not remember the amount at all ? I must put it to you that you only had two gallons left." Whether it would do much good is another matter. It is always possible that the witness in the box is lying or mistaken, but in these sort of cases it is often common sense to assume that he is not.

Now comes the police story—the passing patrol car ; the

boy seen standing by the kerb filling up from a tin; the boy stopping what he was doing; the questioning, the pool of petrol discovered beside an Austin saloon parked down the road; the rubber tube found in the back of the boy's own car, still dripping; the boy's face smelling of petrol. . . .

" Do you want to ask the witness any questions ? "

" You didn't see me go near his car, you didn't see me take any petrol, you didn't see me——"

" *Did* you see him ? " the magistrate asks.

" When we arrived on the scene the accused was standing behind his own car."

" Anything else ? "

The youth shakes his head and sits down again.

" Just one moment, Constable. Did you say you checked *his* tank ? "

" We did, sir."

" How much did you find ? "

" Just under three gallon, sir."

" The owner of the Austin told us that he was *four* gallons short." When the accused stands without a lawyer, the magistrate usually chips in for the defence by putting forward anything that may strike him as being in his favour. (Of course the magistrate has not been briefed, he has not outside knowledge and can only go by what he hears and sees in court during the actual trial.) " How do you account for the discrepancy ? "

" Well, your Worship, there was quite a bit spilt on the ground, it was quite a big pool."

" Over a gallon? I upset the milk the other day, it looked like an awful lot and it was only a quarter of a pint."

A second constable is called who tells the same story word for word.

The youth had thought of a question. " At what temperature," he asks, " does petrol freeze on the ground ? "

The constable doesn't know, the magistrate says that he doesn't know either. " Was it freezing ? "

Summary Justice

"As a matter of fact it was quite a warm night, your Worship."

The inspector steps back. "This is the case for the prosecution." The clerk asks the youth whether he wishes to give evidence on his own behalf. He makes at once for the box but is checked, and told that he has the right to speak from the dock if he so chooses. He looks as if uncertain whether this was offered in order to save the trip; the magistrate explains. "If you remain in the dock, you will not take the oath and I would not be allowed to ask you any questions. If you choose to go into the witness-box, you must take the oath and you may be cross-examined on your story. Which do you choose?" The boy stands as if waiting to hear further pros and cons. A hunted look crosses his face. Then he points, "From over there."

He is asked to tell the story in his own words, and he begins in the middle. Well, yes, it was his father's car—he was driving home. From where? A café—he thought he was running out of juice—he got out his spare tin and filled up—that's what he was doing, that was all there was to it.

There is nothing prepossessing about this youth, yet one wishes it may turn out he hasn't done it. There is something in most of us that longs for things and people to come out right. So we hope that the young man before us has not stood in the dark road pulling the choking liquid to his mouth to scrape fourteen and twopence, is not now lying his sulky way out. But even more we long for the good turn of fate—the happy coincidence, the end that ends well.

The police do not bother to cross-examine; the boy is motioned to walk back into the dock.

The magistrate addresses him. "Well, I have no doubt at all in my mind that you have committed the offence with which you were charged." The illusion is shattered.

The emotional climate of a trial is strange; it breeds a compound of scepticism and faith, an alert weighing of the facts and the sound of the facts, and an ultimate turning to the man in the chair, the more than arbiter, the oracle, the last word. And afterwards, it is a shock to find that one had looked to him to provide the miracle. The third shock is that of course he must be right.

More nemesis steps up. " He's a single man, your Worship, nineteen years of age, he lives with his parents, there are six previous convictions. [Reading] In 1954 by the Juvenile Court for stealing from a gas meter.... In 1955 by the Juvenile Court for taking and driving away a motor-bicycle. . . . In 1956 he was put on two years' probation. . . . In 1958 . . ."

" What was the last one ? " asks the magistrate, who, like the rest of the court, hears it all for the first time.

" In February of this year for breach of probation and taking and driving away a motor-vehicle."

" You are becoming a criminal, you know," says the magistrate.

No answer.

" I want a full report before I can decide what I shall have to do." More work for Mr. Harper, more work for the police. " Remanded in custody for eight days."

The gaoler says, " He asks if he can see his mother."

" Certainly," said the magistrate.

" Number twenty-eight, sir."

A girl : pale, tear-sodden and very beautiful in a rather grand and now unfashionable way. The face of a girl Charlie Chaplin might have succoured in an early silent film. The charge is shoplifting.

" This would have to happen to *me*."

" Do you plead Guilty or Not Guilty ? "

[Proudly] : " Not Guilty."

" Then sit down, madam, and listen to the evidence."

The girl clutches the rail. " I prefer not to sit."

The lady detective had been quite near. " I saw her pick up a brown cardigan and examine it. She held it against herself for size. She carefully folded the garment into

small squares and pushed it under her coat, then she worked it
under her arm. Then she moved to another counter. There
she chose a dark grey cardigan and folded it into tiny
squares. . . . She subsequently went downstairs, I followed
her through the exit and in the street she began to run. I
stopped her, and my colleague called a policeman. The grey
cardigan was found hidden under her coat."

" You lie ! " the girl cries from the dock.

" *Madam.*"

" I hid nothing—she is not speaking the truth."

" Will you be quiet, madam. You are not doing your case
any good."

" They are all against me——"

Police now give formal evidence of arrest. Search revealed
a grey knitted cardigan. The prisoner had £4. 11. 0. on her,
rather more than the price of the article. (Nothing is said,
and nobody asks, about the whereabouts of the first cardigan ;
the brown cardigan has vanished from the case. It often
happens.)

In the box, the girl takes the oath in the Roman Catholic
form. Her name has a Slav ring. She is calmer now. She
only wanted, she says, to see it in the light.

" Then why didn't you simply take it to the window,
madam ? " says the magistrate.

" The window——? "

" You took it *downstairs* into the street ? "

" I wanted to see it in the light."

" There were several windows on that floor."

" I wanted to see it in peace. For the colour. . . ."

" You hid it under your coat ? "

" So that I could look at it . . . They wouldn't have let me,
[desperate and earnest] they always stop you."

She is led back to the dock.

The magistrate breathes something like a sigh. " I am sorry
to say I find the case against you proved. Your story simply
doesn't hold water."

England

" Twenty-six years of age, sir, entered this country in 1948, living by herself. No previous convictions."

" I should like to hear what the probation officer can tell us," says the magistrate. " Miss James——? " The case is put back.

There are more shoplifting charges. Another plea of Not Guilty by a young man accused of slipping a book inside his overcoat. (We are not told the title.) His case is that he had just bought this very same book, a paper-bound, at another stationer's and struck by the coincidence slid it out of his pocket to show it to the friend who was with him; they were standing close to the counter at the time. Another young man in dufflecoat is called in from outside. More or less the same version comes out in driblets.

" Well, as the accused you are entitled to the benefit of the doubt," says the magistrate; " there seem to have been stacks of this work about, and we heard a witness confirm your story—charge is dismissed."

The defendant walks out of the dock unassisted and leaves the court by the front door.

We did not hear his record. A record is only disclosed in the case of a conviction. It strikes one that this drab dismissal was the first acquittal of the day. The dock is now occupied by a seedy-looking individual in early middle-age.

" Two pairs of men's hose," says the male detective employed by Marks & Spencer's.

" w h a t ? " says the magistrates.

" Two pairs of socks, sir."

The defendant says he had been drinking.

Asked, the police officer says, " Yes, I think he *had* been drinking."

" Not enough not to *know* what he was doing? Perhaps enough not to *care* what he was doing? "

A brief list of previous convictions of a trivial nature.

" Doesn't look as if he were an habitual shoplifter? "

" No, sir."

" I'm going to give you another chance, I shall fine you to-day. Mind—it'll be your last one. So try to pull yourself together, don't go on doing these things. Next time they will have to send you to prison. Three pounds."

The defendant moves his lips.

" Anything you want to say ? "

" I'm very sorry it happened."

The gaoler adds, " He wants to know if he can have time to pay ? "

" Yes."

" Three pounds in seven——! "

A constable has been waiting to relate how he saw a man carrying a lady's umbrella through a street in Chelsea. " I proceeded to follow him and he pressed his pace. I stopped him " (after five minutes' stalking) " and I said to him, ' Is this your umbrella ? ' He replied, ' No, I found it.' " The suspect is a clerkish chap in decent pin-stripe, and one begins to wonder. We've all lugged odder things about the streets and often not in clothes half as good as these. " I said to him, ' Why didn't you give it to me ? ' He said, ' I did not see you.' " " I really cannot see where this is leading to, officer," says the magistrate. All the same, a remand is granted. Now comes a woman who accuses her lodger of having made away with two single sheets. He, a curly light-brown, stands waving his hands, uttering soft syllables.

" *Does* he understand English ? "

" Not really, your Worship."

" Then where is the interpreter ? *Why* was no arrangement made ? " The magistrate by now is worn to a thin wire. The case is put back. It takes a moment to get the box clear of the landlady. " Possession of Indian hemp. Inside top, your Worship, stuck to it with tape." A match-box is handed up. It was found on a man arrested in a café brawl. (Everybody is searched on arrest.) The court reporter leans over to his neighbour, a Jamaican law student. " He'll say he knows

43

nothing about it." " I know nothing about it," says the defendant. " I don't smoke it. They must have put it in my pocket." " Trafficking ? " says the magistrate. " Oh, no, sir," says the police officer. Ten pounds fine and thirty shillings cost for the prosecution. And now one of those miserable cases, a man pleading guilty to taking four-pence in coppers and a newspaper off a stand. He is thirty-five perhaps, he has had a fresh shave, his clothes are brushed and pressed to the nines, and he looks at the end of his tether. " I don't know, sir. I don't know myself." A service record ; disability pension ; single. " I understand he suffers from some nervous disorder, sir." " Yes," says the magistrate, " but he mustn't take it out on the news-vendors." A discharge. " I should go and see your doctor if I were you."

Next, a couple of stalls bought at an agency with a cheque on no account. Cheque books, as the bank tells us, should be kept in a place of safety. " I obtained the tickets but did not attend the theatre on that night," says the defendant. The magistrate can hardly trust himself to snap.

Something slipped into a bag, something slid into a pocket, something for nothing, something while the fellow's back was turned—fourteen and eleven from a gas meter, seven pounds from an employer's safe, a quarter of tea and two Mars bars from a self-service counter. " I think we might have that window open a bit ; thank you, Williams." A two-litre Riley car taken and driven from a mews : no licence, ninety pounds' damage, no insurance. " The danger of this kind of thing to the public is appalling." A Lambretta motor-scooter taken at Hammersmith, abandoned in Holland Park (two young men share this feat) ; admonition, a fine. " You knew about this case coming up for three weeks, let me see what you've saved against this day ? How much money have you brought ? " The muffled youth looks nonplussed ; he touches his pocket. " A pound."

Half a broiler chicken and three pocket-handkerchiefs ; four hundred packets of Player's cigarettes ; two wristwatches, a cameo brooch and a lead pencil from a dwelling house ; a man's bicycle off the kerb. . . .

" This is number one sir, Patrick O'Connor."

A dreamer's sensation comes over one. *Déja-vu.* That bloated figure in the dock . . . Must then these shades return ? One can well believe that it goes on for ever ; does it also have to begin all over again ?

" He was charged with being drunk in the street. He's only got eightpence on him, sir, but he says he's going to start work on Monday."

" Well, I'll take a chance, Mr. O'Connor. Seven days to pay."

O'Connor stumbles down, carefree.

The magistrate gets up ; he is gone before we are properly on our feet. The time is twenty minutes past one. " Court adjourned until two-fifteen," says the clerk.

———————

There are eleven of these courts in London alone. Doing this kind of work, sitting—without a break—every day of the year except Sundays and the four Bank Holidays, trying to catch up, trying to get through their lists. The lists are always full. At Lambeth, at Clerkenwell, at Shoreditch and Soho and Fulham and Marylebone, at Tower Bridge, the same daily teamwork, the same processions rounded through the docks, the wheels grinding small and quick.

Once I had started to go, I did not wish to stop. Where else but in these places, such sequence of arranged experience, such brief, but magnified, fragments of the monotonies and surprises of human conduct, such random flashes of exposure, such nutshell views of our conflicts ? where else such condensation of kaleidoscopic offerings ?

Each Metropolitan magistrates' court, police court it used to be called, has two full-time (stipendiary) magistrates who sit alternately. Except Bow Street, which has four. Bow Street and Great Marlborough Street, the most Metropolitan of the courts, London definitely, not London area, are to the magistrature what Paris and Washington are to the diplomatic service. Stipendiaries, unlike the lay justices who sit on most of the country benches and who sit perhaps once a fortnight each, are professionals. (They are appointed by the Crown, on the recommendation of the Lord Chancellor, and must be barristers or solicitors of at least seven years' standing.) Also unlike the lay J.P.s who must be at least a pair, one single stipendiary forms a court, that is he may try cases without additional members on the bench; in fact he is the bench. The appointment is for life, or rather until retirement age. It carries a salary of about £3,800 a year. Which, incidentally, is £600 less than the salary of a County Court judge, a judge who has no criminal jurisdiction (no jurisdiction over a person's liberty) and whose functions are almost entirely concerned with money claims.

Men come to the magisterial bench when they are between forty and fifty, and they stay there. To turn back, to go back to the bar is not practicable; no magistrate so far has been made a High Court judge. A dead-end job then, and one must feel that this should not be so. There is a point when experience becomes self-defeating. That particular compound of pace and pressure and importance and triviality must be fraying or blunting as the years go by. Think of dealing every morning of your life with all those men and women at what to them is an hour of great fear—the responsibility: five seconds' inattention may work an injustice; the helplessness: you don't make the laws, you can't change the people; the repetition!

Each court has a different tone. Some magistrates run theirs like a High Court, some like a regiment. Some pride themselves on their good manners; some maintain an exceptionally cordial relationship with the police. Two or three think and speak like lawyers; the rest are also lawyers, but turned schoolmasters, civil servants or committeemen. At one London court the senior magistrate is a woman. The repertoire, on the other hand, is determined by the neighbourhood. In certain districts the breaches of the peace take place mainly at home—assault, blows between men and wives, mothers and sons, lodger trouble; in others, the emphasis is on the street—betting, soliciting, obstruction, that new bugbear, whether by costermonger's barrow or by motor-car. The traipse of morning-after drunks is ubiquitous but in the West End used to be out-numbered by prostitutes six to one.

III

Notes

All breaches of the law are divided into three. Summary
offences, indictable offences tried summarily, and indictable
offences. The first the magistrates *must* try ; the second they
may try ; the third they *cannot* try. All three come up before
the magistrates.

In practice there is no misdemeanour, felony or crime in
England, from spitting on a bypass to capital homicide, that
is not brought (provided it was found out and attributed to
someone over seventeen) at one stage or another in to a
magistrates' court. For certain things there is no choice at all.
Drunkenness (simple), loitering, soliciting, cruelty to animals,
indecent exposure, playing games in the street, the minor
motoring transgressions, offences against the Shop Acts, these
must be dealt with summarily. But when a minor offence is
punishable by more than three months' prison, the accused
may choose to be tried by a judge and jury. False pretences,
receiving, some forms of assault, some forms of fraud, cruelty
to children, dangerous driving and driving under the influence
come into this category, as do most forms of stealing
(theoretically, a straight theft of a million pounds) but never
house-breaking, even if it involves no more than sixpence
snatched from inside a window-sill. " Do you wish to be
tried in this court. . . ? " the clerk is bound to ask, and the
accused will usually end by muttering, here.

The magistrates' range of sentencing is pretty wide. Their

upper limit is six months prison for any *one* offence, twelve months if two or more offences are charged and proved ; the magistrates may also discharge absolutely, bind over, put on probation or fine anything between a shilling and a hundred pounds. (They cannot pass a sentence of Borstal training as that must be for an indeterminate period between nine months to three years ; but they can convict a young offender and send him to a higher court for such a sentence.) The minimum prison sentence in London is Five Days. The reason for this is a practical one ; country courts with convenient cells may give Two or Three. One Day may be given in London, but the day must end with the sitting of the court. A Nominal Day they call it.

The grave offences must go for trial at Assizes. The list is short and sharp. Besides murder, robbery with violence and treason, there are blackmail, arson, bigamy, buggery, fraud ; coining, procuration, perjury, incest, rape. There is also unlawful carnal knowledge and endangering railway passengers and life at sea. Burglary, house-breaking and shop-breaking, concealment of birth and child stealing may go to Quarter Sessions. However, none of these offences can go anywhere unless they have been sent up—committed—by the magistrates (sitting, not as a court of summary jurisdiction, but as examining justices). No criminal prosecution can take place in the higher courts unless the magistrates have first determined whether there is enough evidence to put an accused on trial. They commit or don't commit. If there is not enough to make a *prima facie* case, they can throw it out. As a rule they do commit.

For one thing the prosecution seldom brings in an entirely footling case ; for another the defendant usually prefers not to show his hand at this stage and reserves his defence, and consequently the examining justices only hear one side. Of course if the accused happened to be not merely hard to prove guilty, but manifestly and demonstrably innocent, he would most likely get up then and there and say something to the effect, " This is all nonsense, you have made a complete mistake, I had nothing to do with this thing. At all material times I was out of the country, I was in America. Here is my passport to prove it."

But alas such unequivocal vindication is not often witnessed in the courts. Mistakes *are* made ; most cases bristle with uncertainties, all leave loose ends, but they are of the kind that exercises the public and the legal mind for fifty years, not the kind that is resolved by fitting in one piece of sudden fact.

Actual committal procedure is very slow. " This is for trial, sir ", sends a kind of distress signal through the court, as now every word a witness says will have to be written down, *in longhand*, read back to him, corrected, signed, and the waste and tedium of the process has to be sat through to be believed. Here is a case.

There had been two remands before it became possible to fix this day. The witnesses have come. They have been waiting outside (unheated entrance hall) since eleven o'clock. The first one has just been called. She is a lady on the threshold of old age, dressed in dowdy-smart clothes, pearls—good pearls—and the kind of toque that is firmly worn from break-fast, noon to night. The prisoner is a slightly built dark boy in a white shirt and shoe-string tie, with a young, alert, bird-like and rather charming face. The witness reads the oath, gives and spells her name, her address and occupation ; she runs a sweetshop in Belgravia. As this is getting under way, a black-coated figure bobs up from the stall where he has been sitting doodling behind a stack of extremely well-named cigars. " Your Worship, I represent the prosecution in this Customs and Excise case ; we are also for trial. With respect, I have three witnesses here this morning [he gives a very mournful look at the clock on the wall]. If your Worship could give an indication——? "

The magistrate follows his look and says, " I am very much afraid I shall not be able to reach you to-day. Your witnesses may of course be released."

Counsel bows. " I am very much obliged to your Worship."
But now a second figure comes quickly to his feet. " I
represent the defendant. I also have my witnesses here—all
exceedingly busy men. I very much doubt—with respect—
whether another date would serve. If I may suggest—if your
Worship could see his way of fitting us in to-day ? "

" I appreciate your difficulty, Mr. Foster," says the magistrate, " but you must see that I *cannot* take you before these
cases, these people are all in custody. [From the ledger]
Would Saturday afternoon help you ? "

Signs of horror from both counsel.

" Apparently not. You know, *I* sit on Saturdays. I suggest
you try to find a convenient date with the clerk outside."

" As your Worship pleases."

The witness meanwhile has been cooling her wits in the
box. She is signed to go on.

" He came into the shop, I thought he was a child, I thought
he was going to buy a bar of chocolate or something, suddenly
he puts up a revolver——"

The clerk says, " Just a moment, madam, not quite so fast
if you please."

The witness stops in her tracks. The magistrate leans over
and explains to her that her statement has to be followed by pen.

" Oh, I see."

" Yes, madam ? " says the clerk.

[A bit off her stride] : " Well, then he said to me——"

The clerk [firmly] : " ' He came into the shop——' ? "

" and suddenly he put a revolver on the counter, it was
covered with a handkerchief, a silk handkerchief, but I could
see the muzzle, I hardly believed my eyes, and he said——"

" One moment——"

" ' Give me your money ! ' I was stunned, I didn't answer.
Then he said——"

" Yes——? "

" ' Oh, come on.' So I whipped up the flap, very quickly,
like this, and it flung off the revolver——"

" and he made for the door—— I ran after him—— I called out to people—— in the street and a man—— a man got hold of a policeman—— They caught him."

" Do you see him here ? "

" Yes," she says, without looking.

" Where ? "

" There."

In due course the evidence is read back. Human speech is not easily caught up with. It comes out something like this :

> " He came into the shop. I thought he was going to purchase something. He suddenly put a revolver on the counter, a handkerchief was placed over it. He said, ' Give me your money.' I was so stunned that I made no answer. He said, ' Oh, come on.' I brought up the flap of the counter, the revolver fell and he made for the door. I followed him into the street where I attracted the attention of passers-by who called the police. I identified the accused in court to-day."

The witness signed this record (the deposition), left the box and was asked to sit down in the back of the court. Two policemen and the man who had passed by were put through the same hoops one after the other. The boy asked no questions, and presently the magistrate wound it up. " I commit you for trial at the Central Criminal Court." The boy pleaded Not Guilty and reserved his defence. The magistrate bound over the witnesses for reappearance at the trial, and added, " And I think it could do no harm at this stage if I said to this lady, she did very well—very well, indeed." Smile ; nod ; a half-bow, half returned. Treasured words.

Now this particular case was brief and simple : facts as plain as a gun, a single criminal act, an eye-witness. In a large number of cases, the evidence is circumstantial and cumulative, often based on books and figures. A really well-laid financial fraud may take days—weeks—to commit for trial. And then there are those multiple breaches of the peace, like Making an Affray to the Terror and Disturbance of H.M.'s Subjects, where the evidence of seven hooligans, their girls, a crowd and a van-load of police has to be sorted out and written down. Or take a charge of living on immoral earnings. In such a case there must be evidence first of all that the earnings were in fact immoral, and second that the accused man lived on them " wholly or in part ". In practice easier said than done. In a case, which was heard piecemeal for a couple of hours a week and then adjourned to the next, the man was the husband, the wife said she was a model, and the police had put a watch on their movements and their basement flat for a number of days from 8 a.m. to midnight. The dictation of that part of the evidence went on and on like this :

Plainclothes-man in witness-box : " On the 8th of November at 2.45 p.m. an unknown man rang the doorbell and was admitted to the premises."

" Unknown to whom? " asked the defendant's solicitor.

" The police officer. The man left at 2.52 p.m. after an interval of seven minutes."

The defendant, who sat in the dock in a new camelhair overcoat, was listening with a bored air. He had been in custody for some weeks.

" At 3.16 p.m. an unknown man was admitted to the premises. He left at 3.29 p.m. after an interval of thirteen minutes.

" At 4.22 till 4.46 p.m. An interval of twenty-four minutes.

" At 4.59 p.m. the defendant's wife came out of the front door with her poodle dog. She walked to the bottom of the street and returned at 5.06 p.m.

" At 5.09 p.m. an unknown man rang the doorbell and was admitted.

" At 5.22 an unknown man rang the doorbell. There was an overlap.

" The first man left at 5.23 p.m. The second man left at 5.52 p.m. after an interval of thirty minutes.

England

"At 6.10 p.m. till 6.21 p.m. At 6.45 p.m. till 7.08 p.m.

"At 7.15 p.m. the defendant rang the bell and was admitted. At 7.45 husband and wife went out together. They took a taxi to the Regency Cinema where they joined the 12/6 queue. In the foyer the wife handed defendant two £1 notes to pay for the tickets. On the 9th of November, at 11.35 a.m.——"

The timetables were interrupted only by one other passage. A police officer had finally rung up the flat himself (telephone number on the card in the corner-shop window). A woman's voice had told him that it was two guineas for personal service. "'How personal?' 'As personal as could possibly be.'" The defence instantly submitted that this piece of evidence was not admissible (telephone and trickery apart, the words came from the accused's own wife). The prosecution maintained that this evidence was the essence of the case.

"Oh, frequently the most relevant evidence is not admissible," said the magistrate. "I will give you a ruling on it next week."

And what of the procedure? Is it really necessary? It is a cardinal maxim of our criminal law that there should be safeguards at all stages of an inquiry; pared to the barest bones, the principle behind committal procedure is that there should be a record of the evidence on which an accusation is based, that this record should be made in the presence of the accused and in public (which raises other points) and before an independent judicial authority, and that this record should be acknowledged, that is checked and signed, in the same open court. And this last makes for the—disputed—technical difficulty, a witness, they say, can only check something he is able to read. He cannot read a shorthand note. (In practice he seldom gets a look at the longhand one either; it is read to him.)

At the actual trial, the depositions are of the greatest usefulness to the lawyers who conduct the case (they are the bases of their briefs), to the trial jury they are of none at all. The judge sees the depositions, the jury does not. The evidence presented to them is oral and direct, the " best available " ; they do not hear the records, but the live witnesses who made them.

The witnesses themselves have no copies of their depositions (although at times they must wish they had). Counsel has them in front of him, and very handy they can be for catching out significant deviations. One has seen it happen, and when it does it often swings the case. More commonly, the deviations are of a footling nature and may just help the defence a little by discrediting a witness's memory ; they often boomerang.

Safeguards at all stages of the criminal investigation. A prosecution is generally set off in more or less this way—something comes to the notice of, or is suspected by the police, or by a private person who makes a complaint to the police. In many cases it is something very simple like somebody's dining-room silver being found missing or a man seen sliding down a drain-pipe in the small hours clutching a heavy suitcase. The police, uniformed or plain-clothes C.I.D. investigate, that is they go about asking questions, looking at things. They may ask whom they like and what they like ; nobody need answer. But innocent people usually do, unless rubbed too much the wrong way ; guilty people answer also, in order to conform or out of garrulity or nerves. (There are no grounds for expecting the run of criminals to behave with especial judgment under strain.) The guilty then may blab or yarn, but not for long. It goes against our popular and legal grain to let a man condemn himself out of his own mouth without at least a warning (a sporting chance), and the judges see to it that he does not. The line where the investigational iceberg emerges into judicial view is when the police, finding their original idea strengthened or confirmed, make up their mind to arrest. From here on, the police are under Judge's Rules, and several things must happen.

First of all, the caution. The police must audibly tell the suspect in the words of the well-known formula that he need not say anything at all but that what he does say may be taken down in writing and used as evidence. This warning may have to be given in the middle of a fascinating tale—mark that the magic moment comes the second the, perhaps listening, police officer in charge has decided on arrest *in his mind*.

As soon as feasible afterwards, the caution must be written down in the exact words that were used, and must be dated, timed, and signed by the suspected person.

Arrest itself is made on warrant. (Unless it happens to be *in flagrante*, in which case the police—and in certain circumstances you and I—may and do arrest without one.) A warrant is obtained by two police officers seeking a magistrate, or a judge—judges being *ex officio* magistrates for the whole of England—in chambers, in court, at home, with a written form stating whom they want to arrest and why. They swear to the truth, the magistrate reads and, if he agrees, he signs. Next, the arrested person must be charged, that is formally accused of a specific offence. He is taken to the nearest police station where an inspector in his presence enters the charge in a book. (Note that hereby the accused has passed into the hands of the uniformed branch of the force: the C.I.D. disposes of no cellars to detain him in.) Unless granted bail by the police, he will spend the night in a station cell. Within twenty-four hours he must be brought before a magistrate in open court. There he will either be tried at once (summarily) or remanded for another date. There will have to be a date. Limited, as we have seen, to eight—renewable—days if the accused is to remain in custody. If so, he will not be sent back to a police cell, but taken to a local prison which will be under the control of the Prison Service. And in such a prison he will remain until his trial. Note, that from the point of his first being brought before a magistrate, he is no longer available for any questioning by the police or any other agent of the prosecution. Note also, that in some other countries it is at this point, after arrest, that the questioning gets properly under way.

A rule of law is a *sine qua non* of any tolerable material life. The very next question is, what law? Twenty-four hours from arrest to court is a good law; our Judges' Rules, which are not strictly speaking law, are good rules; good not just for some of us against an evil day, but for all of us, good in concept and in practice. Handsome stays who handsome does. A society which will self-restrict its means of dealing with burglars and suspected persons is in less danger of being trapped or lulled or bullied into losing its liberties than a society which does not mind if someone in a corner uses arbitrary power against its enemies.

Good rules only live as long as there are custodians. Never take anything for granted; not long ago I heard a rather wide-awake magistrate swoop on the droning from the witness-box:

" . . . at the North-East corner of the Queen's Road at 4 a.m. yesterday, your Worship, I proceeded——"

" 4 *a.m.*? " (I had noticed nothing amiss.)

" 4 a.m., sir."

" Then w h y was he not brought here *yesterday?*" and the fat—behind the scenes—was in the fire.

There are, obviously, good judges and magistrates and exceptionally good judges and magistrates and, what we might call, not so good judges and magistrates. But good—apart from the fact that we all know a clear-minded, fair and able man when we see one and are delighted with what we see—good in relation to what, good to what end? A judge on the criminal bench is a man who administers the law which he has not made; he may do worse or he may do better, but he cannot do very much better than this law; and the rule of law itself is not an absolute, not a mystique, but a contract between men. It is an instrument of society : our instrument. What then do we think we want? Maintenance of our present fabric of living, standardisation, protection, certainly ; but we do not all agree on the extent, the means or the price. Moreover this straightforward matter of expediency is immensely complicated by our simultaneous concept of justice—which may well be a mystique—by our impulse towards a disinterested sorting out of right and wrong. The common law is unentangleable from the moral law.

Either is capable of strange twists. Our actual laws, and the penalties for breaking them, were evolved through centuries in a tortuous course during which almost every argument has been put forward to legislate for almost anything. Do we know much more now ? Are we any kinder ? Looking at the criminal investigation of the past, we might say yes. But we are also more hard-pressed, mostly by sheer numbers— too many sheep in the pen—and by the speed of events, out-run by-the scientific revolution.

We are shocked also—many of us—by the retributive methods inherited from an immediate past. We are very uneasy about the death penalty ; we are becoming more and more uneasy about prison. Should penalties be merely deterrents ? Do deterrents deter ? We set up commissions, we spend a little on schools, we look at statistics from Sweden. Many people would no longer say they were *for* prison ; they might say, but how could we do without, what should we do ? Sentencing, sending a man, to prison is a fearful thing ; then so are many forms of crime. What should we do indeed— assuming that what we roughly agree to want is a reasonably safe society maintained without injustice or oppression and a minimum of inflicted suffering—what *can* we do ? Perhaps the first answer cannot be any immediate or concrete solution but a state of mind. Watch and learn, think, not shy from change ; make mistakes and learn again. Admit wrongs. Is it too late ? Is it too soon ?

Notes

I once asked a, professional, magistrate what he considered to be his first duty. " The keeping of the peace," he said, " and the rehabilitation of the individual. They go together. Although sometimes there is conflict . . ."

The good magistrate, one might say, must be a good man. And possibly a contented one. He ought not to be too highly-strung ; a man with a Dostoevsky view of life would wear himself to a frazzle in six months. (Dickens of course would have done splendidly, in his youth at least.) As a barrister put it, " Oh, a happily married chap, you know ; garden, kind heart, good health and not too much out for himself." Another magistrate named the qualities, in that order : " Humanity ; common sense ; humility ; a little law, a very clever chap would be wasted ; a sense of humour." To which one might add, imagination, some experience of life and an ability to absorb the unexpected.

The not-so-good magistrate is a man who talks with his head down, who seldom takes his nose out of the ledger. He does not look at the people who speak to him. He hurries them along with hnhn's and well's. He interrupts witnesses and when there is counsel he takes the examination out of his mouth. He browbeats young barristers. He gives everybody a sense of the scarcity of his time. He does not appear to listen. He pretends to be unable to understand what people say to him. He is sarcastic when it is too easy. He makes up his mind, or appears to have made up his mind, at the beginning of a case. He loses his temper not because it might be necessary, but because he loses it. He loses it, not because he has been tried beyond endurance, but because it is a cherished exercise. He shows contempt for his customers and his place of work, and he betrays his sense that he is made of different clay.

A judge's or a magistrate's most telling power is over the man or woman convicted of their second or third or fourth offence. It is here that choice comes in. The extreme limits of the scale present no dilemma, the man who sells fruit off a costermonger's barrow in a restricted street, the man charged with murder. A first offender is very often let off. A second offender's position is more precarious, already there is more danger in the future and less hope. Fewer first offenders become second offenders than second offenders become third offenders, to put it in an Irish bull. And it is here that a sentence can make or break.

What can one expect to happen in practice? In a morning we saw a great many people fined, two or three discharged; we did not hear a single prison sentence. A number of cases were left dangling. They were put back or remanded for a report. What happens to those people?

First there was the listless man, number twenty-two, who had taken forty-eight books of matches and a piece of cake from the seat of a motor-car. He will be sent up again as soon as the court resumes after the luncheon adjournment. He will have been given some kind of a meal—put together by the matron—tinned beans and a fried egg, and certainly a cup of tea. He could have smoked, if he had a cigarette, that is. The cell will have been cold. The magistrate himself may not have left the building, there's sure to have been business, papers to sign, applications to read; besides, where could he go? A magistrate at Bermondsey or Islington is a lonely man. Not for him the gregarious life of the courts and inns, the masculine midday jollity at the well-served counters of Fleet Street and the Strand, the grill-room of the Law Society, the judges' common-room lunch; if *he* were to put his nose around the corner all he might run into would probably be O'Connor. At two fifteen, then, everybody will be back in court. Mr. Harper, the probation officer, may go straight into the witness box. This man, doing his difficult, balanced duty, may say, " Well, I talked to him, sir. There isn't a great deal I could get out of him. It seems he's been over here since Christmas and he hasn't been able to find regular work. He says he's had bronchitis . . . He's had *some* relief; he doesn't seem to be clear what he's entitled to. He doesn't seem to care . . . I asked him if he would like to go back to Ireland, he says he doesn't know. He thinks his people have moved. I caused inquiries to be made. . . ."

The magistrate may do one of various things. He may decide to have the court pay Kelly's fare to Ireland (London courts have funds ; it's the local poor box). He may remand him in custody for a mental and physical report, a thing people rather dread. He may make a probation order which would give Kelly someone to lean on for a year or two. What *is* certain is that George Kelly will not be sent to prison and that the court will help him in his next few steps.

Then there will be a reappearance of the girl with the drowned Garbo look who told the court that she had put the cardigan under her coat because she wanted to see it in the light. Miss James's report may run something like this : " She seems to be very much distressed by what she has done, she says she cannot understand it. I tried to talk to her about her earlier life, she came to this country when she was fifteen years of age . . . Her family were killed. I understand a Catholic organisation helped her through a secretarial school . . . She now holds a good position. She's inclined to think that everyone's against her . . . *I* think she's lonely, sir."

The magistrate will speak a very grave warning and order a conditional discharge.

And what about the youth who pleaded Not Guilty to siphoning petrol from a tank ? He will be up again in eight days, looking just the same, peaked, in his neat suit, his hair smarmed down, and the reports will have come in. They may be fairly good, bad or indifferent.

A decent home, on the strict side. ". . . he was always hard to control, the other children never gave us any trouble, his father used to——" Or perhaps, " I'm afraid, sir, he's been under rather bad influence, there's no home supervision." Employer ? " There have been quite a few, sir, he left school at fifteen ; he was dismissed from his last job." Or just as possibly, " His foreman has only good to say of him, he's well liked at his place of work." A probation order ? " Well, sir, as you remember, there's been breach of probation before . . . His last officer doesn't sound very hopeful. . . ."

Quarter Sessions then for a sentence of corrective training ; or—this could be one of the cases in which a remand in custody, a week in the cells, is handled as a small deterrent— a dressing down and a stiff fine that will take the cigarettes and cinema out of his wage packet for a month or two, and another chance.

And afterwards ? Later, when it's all over and done with ? One does not know. If one had to prophesy one might say, the girl will not come back. Whether she'll be able to get reconciled to life is another question. George Kelly a free man again, whatever that may mean to him, will shift along, shift being the word, not doing any great harm, not doing himself much good. As for the boy, well, one might say that the boy has got more time. The boy may be a company director yet.

The Worst We Can Do

Not the worst. Not about the great wrongs. Not about bad laws. Not about Adolph Beck or Chessman or judicial errors ; not about hanging or flogging or the Labouchere Amendment. About the small things men do to each other every day if they have the power and the lack of imagination, or if their convictions happen to run that way. It goes unrecorded, it is hardly noticed, but it lives on in the memories of those concerned.

Here are a few incidents, taken almost at random. All occurred within the same three weeks in various places, which shall be nameless, up and down the country.

This was at Quarter Sessions. It was the morning of the first day and a number of accused persons were being put up in the dock one after the other and asked what they were going to plead. This is done so that the court may have some idea as to the timetable, as a plea of Not Guilty may take a whole day or more to try as against the half hour or hour of a plea of Guilty. It was the turn of a girl, a foreign girl, charged with being an accessory in a case of larceny. She pleaded Not Guilty, and was told that her trial would come on two or three days later in the week. As so far she had been out on bail, her counsel rose and asked the chairman of the Sessions for an extension for these last few days. The chairman turned to the police officer in charge of the case.

The police officer said, " No objection to bail, sir."

The chairman said, " I see that she has left her address, she's no longer in the same place."

Counsel had not heard about this, and the girl explained. She had had rather a row with her landlady last night, she was moving on to somewhere else.

" Well, in that case . . ." said the chairman.

The police officer said distinctly, " We have no objection to bail, sir, we believe she means to turn up."

" She hasn't got family or anything in this country ? " said the chairman. " I mean it's not going to break up her life if she spends a night or two in Holloway—will it ? Very well—" Counsel opened his mouth— " Bail not extended." The girl gave one gasp, opened *her* mouth and was wiped away.

At this same Sessions several courts were sitting at the same time ; I happened to come into one of them towards the end of a case. It was a house-breaking affair and involved three brothers. Counsel for the youngest was just beginning to address the bench in mitigation. He was pleading for a probation sentence. " Not really a bad lad—first offence—outside influences——" The chairman of the bench, a Major Blank, interrupted. " Mr. White, I don't want to break into your argument, I only wanted you to know that you are preaching to the converted : this is quite obviously a case for probation. The court has already decided on it. I thought that you—and your client—would be glad to know."

Counsel said, " I *am* very much obliged to you, sir." This is of course an incidental example rather of the good we can do. Indeed, the effect on people of such moments is magical. I remember another like it, only more so, in that same fortnight. A very old High Court judge was sitting at another Quarter Sessions. He had been taking a plea of Guilty in a rather fantastic case of a man who had suddenly gone wild and

obtained money under false pretences—just to pay for hotel
bills and shows and clothes and be able to move on—ninety
times in the course of a year. A girl—with him in the dock—
was involved also, and the man spoke up for her very nicely.
He alone, he said, was to blame, he had started the whole
thing, he dragged her along, she had been unwilling and
miserable all the time—he felt very badly about her, all the
more so as if he ever was a free man again he would go
back to his own wife. (The wife was in court, too, and
spoke up for *him*; it was all round a most magnanimous
occasion.) As the bench was about to withdraw for delibera-
tion, the old judge said to the girl, "I might as well tell
you at once, madam, that we do not intend to send you to
prison."

And that of course was what did happen. When sentence
was eventually pronounced it was probation for the girl—
Good luck, she said to the man, Good luck to you, he said,
as she was being moved away—and three years for him, and one
can be sure that he went to prison with a lighter heart and a
better chance because of that judge's way.

But to return to Major Blank. Or rather *not* to return to
him. I had meant to spend the rest of the day in his court.
The first case on the list after the luncheon adjournment was
a homosexual plea of Guilty (not between consenting adults);
when the time came however, word arrived that the chairman
of the Sessions had decided to take the case himself. It was
moved to the court of the man I had heard opening the
Sessions. It was a distressing case. A high member of the
clergy had sent a letter pleading for a probation sentence.
A woman with an academic appointment went into the box
herself and pleaded the same. A psychiatrist had written to
say that prison would be disastrous for that man. He was
married, there was one child, another was on the way. The
wife was in court, ready to do what she could. Counsel for the
defence put his plea in mitigation well; counsel for the
prosecution was reasonable. The police said, "He's been

England

very helpful, sir, he couldn't have been more helpful." The bench was out for twenty minutes. Their decision was a long prison sentence.

It is seldom that an English judge or magistrate does not at least wince or yawn when a psychiatric opinion is being read ; often he speaks his mind. This is a favourite. " It is not going to hurt your victim any the less to know that you knocked her down because of some complex or other." True. Just as it is not going to hurt any the less if what knocked her down had been a falling branch or brick. We no longer think of cutting down the tree or burning down the house, we've become quite rational towards inanimate things. The tree may need a prop, those bricks may need more mortar, the hooligan may need some treatment or another kind of life, the chief difference is that we know more about roofs and trees, men and women being of course more complex, and we much less willing to learn.

Then there was a case tried by a lay bench. Lay benches—in some ways—are more relaxed. Some sit at ten, some at half past, some at a quarter to eleven. The bench more often than not is ten minutes late coming on. Nobody minds. " Good morning, Mr. Mortlock." " Good morning to you, chief inspector." " Hallo Bill." " Hallo, Hugh." They talk about the hay ; they talk about the time it took them on the road ; they talk about the morning's work. " Two Dangerous-or-Careless," answers the clerk, " and one Exposure." " Mine won't take long," says the solicitor whose face is seen at every session in the district, " I'm pleading Guilty." " You A. E. Horne, Bob ? " " I'm prosecuting." The young man from the County Gazette wants to get the local names right ; someone at the clerk's table spells them out for him, the police constable supplies an address.

Someone shouts, " Rise ! " Everybody scrambles to his feet and place, and in they file : the chairman first, followed by the lady on the bench, followed by one, or two, or three more men. They are bowed to, nod back, scrape their chairs ; the clerk takes up his papers, the business of the day is getting under way. One can look at their faces.

Here, the pendulum swing between excellence and the opposite is wider. Members of the legal profession have certain standards, lay justices, also, have standards but they are more fluctuating and individual, and there is on the whole a greater tendency to give free, self-righteous rein to one's own convictions. To this some lay benches of course are notable exceptions ; even in my own most limited experience I have come across at least one lay bench—out of perhaps twenty—neither at Oxford nor at Cambridge, that appeared to be a model of humanity, good sense and charitable worldliness. I recall one case in which this bench also displayed professional legal fairness. A man was charged with driving a motor-car without third-party insurance ; he himself had firmly believed his car to have been insured at the material time and it became quite clear from the evidence that the whole thing was due to some clerical muddle or negligence in the insurance broker's office and to nothing else. The bench—three men, one woman—withdrew for a few minutes, then the chairman regretfully announced that there would have to be a conviction as the defendant was technically guilty of the charge (having *de facto* driven a car without insurance). Now a conviction need not necessarily be followed by a penalty, and indeed a discharge was in the air, when the chairman was interrupted by the citation of the previous convictions. There was a string of them, all in motoring, all over the last two years, three for speeding, one for careless, one for dangerous driving. The members of the bench looked at each other, whispered a few words, then the chairman said, " This *is* a bad record. However, speeding and dangerous driving have nothing to do with the present offence. An absolute discharge."

England

The clerk asked, " Endorsement ? "
The chairman said, " No."

The chairman of another bench set much store by people saying they were sorry. The kindly gaoler was wont to tip the prisoners off; in consequence whenever that bench sat the court would ring with parrot cries from the dock, " I'm very sorry, I'm very sorry, sir, I'm sorry."

In another district, a punctuating cry would come from the bench itself. That chairman was much affected by anything involving material loss or damage. " There's property at stake," he would cry against whatever was being explained to him. " Man, there's property at stake ! "

The case I want to describe was that of a woman who pleaded Not Guilty to stealing half a pound of butter from a self-service store in a small town. She was a woman under forty, of respectable middle middle-class, married, with grown-up children. She was dark and small, and on that day she looked distracted.

This is what had happened. The store detective had observed her putting one half-pound package of butter into the store's official basket and a second half-pound into her own shopping bag. He watched her going out, and saw that at the gate she paid for the things in the store basket only. Outside, he stopped her. According to his evidence, she said to him, " I don't know why I did it." According to hers, he gave her such a shock, began at once to bully and to threaten, that she had no idea of what she might have said. According to the evidence of both, she had a sort of collapse and was taken back into the store for a glass of water. The police arrived and she was taken to the local station.

The police evidence was that she had been very much upset, almost out of her mind. She readily made a statement. It tallied in every way with the evidence she gave at the trial. She went into the box and poured out her story. She had, she told the court, received the very morning of that day a

The Worst We Can Do

letter from her brother in Ireland. (The letter was found on her by the police, and was given in evidence.) Her poor father, the best man in the world, whose health had been giving anxiety for some time, had taken a sudden turn for the worse, he had been taken to hospital a few hours ago, her brother wrote, and his state was very grave. The news had made her feel beside herself with anxiety and grief; she and her husband had made arrangements for her to leave for Ireland in the afternoon, he was to drive to where she could catch a train to the coast, she was going to straighten up the house for him—there had been a dozen things to see to and she unable to put her mind on one of them.

She had gone out to arrange for leave of absence from her job (she held a post at a local institution), after that she went to the store to get a few things to tide her husband over, tea, sugar, bacon, butter. She then remembered that a neighbour had asked her the night before to get a half-pound of butter, she supposed it must have been this that made her slip that second half-pound into a different bag, some idea of keeping them apart, though she had not really thought of anything, except of her poor dear father. . . . And then that man came after her in the street—he was dreadful—the shock of it—I could have died. Me! steal something! I've never taken a penny that did not belong to me in all my life, ask anyone in my family, there isn't one of us who wouldn't rather die!

"When you left the store," said the chairman, "you paid for a quarter of a pound of tea, one pound of sugar, a quarter of a pound of bacon, one package of chocolate biscuits and, you say you thought, for two half-pounds of butter. And yet the total on your pay slip only came to six shillings and eleven pence. Did you not think that six and eleven was rather a small amount for tea, sugar, bacon, biscuits and a whole pound of butter?"

"It might have been elevenpence or sixteen and eleven for all I'd have noticed that morning!"

Counsel for the defence said that husband and wife were very comfortably off, he was a businessman with a good job, she filled a decently-paid post, they owned their house. He called evidence as to character: a life of blameless respectability— no such thing as a previous conviction—thirteen years in the same place. The head of her department gave evidence.

" And did Mrs*** duties involve the handling of sums of money? "

" Yes."

" Of valuables, or jewellery ? "

" Oh, yes. Constantly."

" Was there ever any complaint ? anything missing ? "

" Never to my knowledge. That is, in the three years I've been there. But when I took over I was given to understand that she had the highest reputation."

" Would you call Mrs.*** a woman of undoubted honesty? "

" I would."

The bench retired for about ten minutes. On their return the chairman announced, " We find the offence proved. A fine of two pounds."

V

The Domestic Side

Magistrates' courts have another side which in London comes
into its own in the early afternoon. People appear to answer
charges brought against them by their neighbours, to discuss
their means or to be reconciled to their wives. Although the
magistrates cannot grant a divorce, their matrimonial jurisdiction covers a good deal of the remaining ground. They
have power to make out separation and non-cohabitation
orders, maintenance orders and affiliation orders, that is
power to compel a man to support his wife, his children and
his bastards. They can over-ride a parent's refusal to allow
a minor child to marry, and they preside at proceedings
known as matrimonials.

Matrimonials are held in Closed Court with the gallery
seats cleared and the press forbidden to report ; most people
would still call them public. There are present, besides the
magistrate, the contending couple and the clerk, half a dozen
policemen in their various functions, possibly some social
worker or law student, a probation officer and an usher.
No disclosures are barred.

" He's been sleeping in the garage for the last fortnight,"
the wife says from the witness-box.

" Only because *she's* been so nervous——"

The magistrate is not trying so much to apportion who was
right or wrong but to sort the general situation and find out
what the parties really want and whether what they want may

still be feasible. He will say, and not for the first time, " Will
you be silent, Mr. Jones. You will be able to tell your story
presently. First we hear one side, then we hear the other, as it
has gone on for fifteen hundred years."

" You were at me all the time," the husband has turned
directly to his wife. " I have my job to think of, your own
mother said——"

" How dare you bring in mother ? It was *you* who said to
me the day we were going to get Johnnie's coat and you had
kept the alarm clock——"

" *Madam*," says the magistrate, " will you *please* address
your evidence to me."

" If he says I locked the front door he's a liar."

" I think we can leave the locking of the door out of it for
the moment," says the magistrate, " though of course if it was
in fact locked, and I am not prepared to say that it is in any
way proved that it was not so locked, that would be a very
grave matter indeed. Now I understand you to say, Mr.
Jones, you are willing to return to your wife, and you, Mrs.
Jones, to have him back——"

"I said we ought to make another go of it for the children's
sake, but not if she——"

" Not if he——"

The magistrate will now try to begin again in the middle.
And if and when Mr. and Mrs. Jones eventually decide to
call it a day, it will be he who has the children's custody to
think about.

" *Arrears* of £8. 15. 0., sir, from an order of 10/- a week for
the wife and 15/- for a child made in 1948."

This order is a maintenance order, and this is how it comes
into being. A man goes off ; the wife applies to the court, the
court summons the husband, tries to find out about his earnings
and general circumstances, then makes out an order to pay
so and so much a week to the wife, so much for each child.
(If the man chose not to turn up, it would amount to contempt

of court and a warrant of arrest might be made out eventually. He could try to disappear. It is no longer easy.) The money must be paid weekly into court; the women come and call for it at the pay office. No order is immutable. The man may come to earn less, a child grow to need more, grow up; the wife may marry again. Either party can apply for a change of order. On the other hand a day may come when the man hasn't paid because he won't or can't, and he is summoned for what is called arrears.

In a lounge-suit, folded overcoat on his arm, he stands before the bar—*outside* the dock—and says he is a man's hairdresser's assistant and business has been bad.

" ? ? "

" Well, sir, for us it was. People want less haircuts in the cold weather." Now things are looking up again. How long does he think it will take him to catch up ? He could, he says he's sure, manage another pound a week above the usual.

" Adjourned for four weeks : pay or appear." The magistrate marks his register. " You understand, Mr. Roberts, if you pay regularly every week, you need not come. [Touch of bonhomie : Mr. Roberts is one of the rarer birds] We don't want to see *you*, we want to see your money." Brief smile ; dismissal.

The next is an elderly man owing several weeks on an order of 17/- for a wife. He says he is an outdoor salesman, making £7 a week and not always. He is of a difficult age and visibly on his uppers. Adjourned for fourteen days. Then come a number of men who have been ill. Some brought medical certificates, some did not. Then men who for one reason or another haven't been able to work. Let us switch courts and see a not-so-good magistrate deal with one of them.

" What's he do ? "

Clerk : " He's a window cleaner, your worship."

" Plenty of windows . . . My trouble is getting you fellows to show up."

England

The defendant says he hasn't been able to work in February because of the weather. "Frost and fog," he mutters.

Magistrate: "It won't do you any good to tell silly lies. We've had no rain at all in February."

"We couldn't go out to work, sir, not for three weeks we couldn't——"

"You *heard* [the purpling face, the swelling neck] it didn't rain AT ALL in February."

The clerk, with great courage: "He said frost and fog, sir."

"What?"

"He did not say rain."

"Ah, well—adjourned for a week."

"This is an application for cessation of order, sir."

A young man tries to explain the position. He is paying 25/- a week on an affiliation order. Things have been getting a bit on top of him, he's only earning £5. 10. himself, it's an apprenticeship; now the girl who's had this child by him has got married, the husband is willing to adopt the child. . . .

"Once the child is adopted," says the magistrate (we *are* back in another court), "the responsibility of the natural father comes to an end."

The young man is not quite easy in his mind.

"Yes——?" says the magistrate.

He would get married himself one day and then perhaps *his* wife would, perhaps he might persuade her . . . Oughtn't he to——?

"No, no, no," says the magistrate. "The child will be best with the mother, it's the best all round."

Next a working man in working clothes. "Arrears for £23. 7. 6., sir, from an order of 7/6 for the wife and 10/- for a child made in 1958."

"Is that correct, Mr. Thompson?"

"I don't think that it is."

The magistrate is not having any. "Very well. Then please go outside to the accounts' office and see for yourself."

The Domestic Side

Time is filled by calling a Mr. Hilbert. The name resounds without.

" No appearance," says the constable at the door.

" No appearance, sir, not served." The summons has failed to find Mr. Hilbert.

" So marked," says the magistrate.

Thompson is back and concedes the £23. 7. 6.

" Well, why haven't you paid ? "

He's been out of a job.

" Come and tell us about it from the witness-box."

Thompson is marched over and swears to tell the whole truth.

" You haven't paid for—twenty-three weeks I make it, is that right ? Everybody seems to be better at figures than I am . . ."

" Twenty-three weeks, sir," says the clerk.

" Let me see, this order was made in 1958 . . . *You haven't paid anything at all* ? "

No reaction.

" Out of a job all that time ? "

" You know how it is, your Honour, the building trade——"

" May I see your yellow card ? "

" What yellow card ? "

" The card from the Labour Exchange, aren't you getting unemployment relief ? "

[Tone of self-congratulation] " I've never been near the Labour Exchange in my life."

" What have you been living on ? "

[Wooden-faced, yet smug] " My married daughter."

" How do you expect your wife and child to live ? "

" There's plenty of ways."

" On National Assistance ? At public expense ? "

" There's others what do it."

" Thompson, I'm not going to waste any more time over you. Adjourned for two weeks : pay or serve warrant."

And if Thompson *will not* pay, the last answer is prison from where he *cannot* pay. It's our old friend, the deterrent; a gamble.

———————

There used to be two features of the London courts which were unique; nothing like them could be seen anywhere else in the entire world; they were the prostitutes and the motorists.

With the passing of the Street Offenders' Act in 1959, the prostitutes have vanished from our sight; it may be worth recording their passage while memory is still fresh. The motorists are still with us.

Every morning at half past ten at Bow Street and Great Marlborough there took place a quick parade.

" This is number one, sir, Katherine Seaton."

An ample negress in a grass-green hat climbs the steps.

" Katherine Seaton you are charged with being a common prostitute and with causing annoyance in a public place by soliciting."

[Businesslike] " Guilty."

" Three previous convictions here this month, sir."

The magistrate fixes a vacant stare on the dock. " You admit the previous trouble ? "

Nod.

[Back in ledger] " Want to say anything about it ? "

" No."

" Forty shillings."

" Mary Cheam——" A tall girl, not very young, in a sober tailormade and well-done hair. One would have taken her for a saleswoman in a good London shop.

" Here frequently ? "

" She is, sir."

" You admit that ? "

76

The Domestic Side

" Oh, many times."

" Forty shillings."

A tufted apparition such as one used to see in Curzon Street
after 10 p.m. " Another regular? Pay forty shillings."
On they come—step up, forty shillings, step down, through
the door, up the next, on stiletto heels, in slippers, in well-
polished brogues, in riding boots, and you cannot tell what
you may see next.
A red-wristed housewife in a shapeless cardigan, " She's
been here twice last week, sir.". . . . . . A slim girl in stove-pipe
slacks. . . . . . A tart who looks like a tart. . . . . . A neat
lady from Japan, " Why didn't she appear yesterday? "
" She went to Marylebone by mistake, your Worship."
" Funny, many people seem to do that.". . . . . . Now a nearly
old woman, scraggy, fierce, with kohl around her eyes. . . . . .
An Italian slut with a horse's mane, dressed in three tones
of red. . . . . . An English slut. . . . . . A girl in day-clothes
turned out like a smart débutante, " Why didn't you come
yesterday? " " I suppose I overslept." " Forty shillings and
forfeit of bail.". . . . . . A negro girl with a squashy face but
beautifully made. . . . . . A sagging drab sharing the dock with
a man, an Arab who looks disgusted, " Sexual intercourse
against the railings, your Worship." " A Hyde Park Lady? "
smile to the clerk; " Any money on them? ". . . . . . A girl
with spectacles. . . . . . A flaming blonde, " Why didn't *you*
come yesterday? This has got to stop, you know." [Squarely]
" I didn't have the money yesterday.". . . . . . A girl in
conventional riding kit on her way, presumably, to the
Park. . . . . . A dumpy young thing in blue serge with a silly
pretty face, [Sharply] " How old is she? " " She says seventeen, sir." " Oh. Ever been here before? " " Bow Street,
sir." " I'd like her to have a talk with the probation officer.". . . .
A Jamaican, also young, smiling politely. . . . . .
Furs; touches of tulle; a dressing-gown that might just
pass for an overcoat; tight black frocks and painted lips;

77

house-dress calico. Hair dark at the roots, silk kerchiefs, a dotting of spring hats. Women barely roused from sleep; women in full rig; women with trousers slopping about their ankles under the mackintosh; one or two women of well-bred, well-groomed chic.

All in all it was a curious traffic. The fines collected are said to have come to thirty thousand pounds a year.

————————————

As for the motorists . . . At the fag end of the day, the last of the afternoon, when the court's pulse is at an ebb and the magistrate's cuffs have wilted, when the witnesses have stood down and the defendants are at home or in their cells, and for lack of interest the public gallery lies deserted, it is then at the declining hour that, like the monks and priests in the empty chapel after the long service leaning back in their stalls to their ordered chant, the magistrate and his men settle down to their last litany, the traffic summonses.

For the motorists do not appear.

Traffic summonses in our enlightened times can be dealt with by post. All a motorist charged with a (minor) offence need do is to write a letter—he pleads guilty by mail. This must be one of the rare instances in which the processes of bureaucracy actually contribute to create less work.

The clerk intones:

" Victor Gramsby of Long Hinton Suffolk for causing obstruction of the highway——"

A police officer picks it up:

" On October 16th last index number ADT 999 in Old Compton Street from six fifteen to six fifty-five p.m., your Worship, for forty-five minutes——"

Second police officer's voice carries on:

" I pointed out the offence to him and told him he would be reported. He said, ' Oh.' "

The clerk cuts in, reading:

78

The Domestic Side

" ' I had an important engagement, I did not see a No Parking sign, I only intended to leave it for a few minutes.' "

The magistrate's voice :

" Twenty shillings."

Third policeman's voice.

" Twenty shillings." He enters it in a book.

The clerk :

" For causing obstruction——"

" On 14th September last " (mark the date : the traffic summonses are the orphans of the lists, always six months behind), in Clifford Street——"

" He said, ' I only left it for a few minutes, there are plenty of other cars here, why don't you report them ? ' "

" Twenty shillings."

" . . . . in Bouverie Street ; traffic was reduced to a single line ; one hour and ten minutes."

" ' I am unfamiliar with this part of the city, I had to see an important customer, I did not think I would leave it for long.' "

" Thirty shillings."

Traffic lights : " ' I was sure the lights were amber.' " " Twenty shillings." Exceeding the speed limit : " ' There were other cars in front of me doing more, it was after a long wet drive.' " " Forty shillings and licence endorsed." Obstruction : " ' I had an important engagement, I had been driving about looking for a place, I only left it for a short period.' " " Twenty shillings." No light on a bus route : " ' It worked perfectly that morning.' " " Twelve and six-pence." Obstruction : " ' I found I had to obey a call of nature.' " " Fifteen shillings." Speed limit : " ' I had been taking my mother-in-law to hospital.' " " Twenty shillings and endorsement." Obstruction : " ' I must point out that I belong to a law-abiding family, three of my brothers are vicars and another is a superintendent in the Metropolitan Police Force.' " " Twenty shillings."

The motorists are not seen, there is no procession ; but as

letter is folded up on letter, there passes through this court the same thin trail of human frailty. " ' My watch must have stopped.' " " ' I went there on my employer's orders.' " " No excuse given."

The magistrate says, " Unusual. One might say, refreshing. *What* ? Nothing at all ? *No* mitigation of the offence ? "

" None, your Worship."

" Three pounds."

PART TWO

GERMANY

I

Karlsruhe:
The Case of Dr. Brach

The law, the working of the law, the daily application of the law to people and situations, is an essential element in a country's life. It runs through everything; it is part of the pattern like the architecture and the art and the look of the cultivated countryside. It shapes, and expresses, a country's modes of thought, its political concepts and realities, its conduct. One smells it in the corridors of public offices, one sees it on the faces of the men who do the customs. It all hangs together whether people themselves wish or acknowledge it or not, and the whole is a piece of the world we live in.

One way to get to know it is to travel. Go and look, see for oneself, get hold of a little, make a guess at the whole. It is not a very complete way; for the lay spectator, the non-lawyer, the stranger, it is about the only way. What one takes home may not amount to much, but it is all one can get; in our astronomically complex environment many of us must learn to resign ourselves to nibbling or never never know anything at first hand at all.

All the same, something had kept me back for years. It seems all right somehow for the amateur to go to China and to Florence or down the Amazon, to look at the Prado or at Russia. He may even write about it. For the desire to travel and the desire to write spring from the same instinct, and he who has it cannot follow one without the other. But when

Germany

it comes to the amateur, the private unlearned aficionado of the law, to set out cold on a tour of Western European law courts, it hardly seems legitimate. Lawyers stare and laymen shrug. Nevertheless, uneasy and much aware of my unprofessional limitations, I went. Justice is supposed to be seen being done, and this must surely mean seen also by the likes of us. Besides, the lawyers do not have the time.

One October morning—Monday morning at 8.45 a.m., for such I understood were Continental hours—and a fine day, I found myself outside the High Court of Justice at Karlsruhe, Germany. Karlsruhe used to be the capital of the Grand-Duchy of Baden and the residence of the reigning Duke until 1918 and the fall of all German monarchy, when it became the capital of a not very convinced republic. Baden—the Black Forest; the universities of Heidelberg and Freiburg; Baden-Baden, the favourite spa in its time of the St. Petersburg *beau monde*; saw-mills for the rest, vineyards, leather, small-scale farming and a very near border with French Alsace—a mainly rural land, had long been regarded as a slow and sleepy backwater, looked upon by the inhabitants themselves with some complacence as the Deep South of Germany —such things are always relative—and after the last war it ceased to continue on its own and became joined to its more industrialised and prosperous neighbour, the former Kingdom of Würtemberg. It is now the smaller part of a state of the Federal Republic, the name is Baden-Würtemberg, the capital Stuttgart. To compensate Karlsruhe for its lost status, it was made the law capital of Western Germany. In addition to the courts of summary jurisdiction and the high courts of first instance of a German provincial capital, it has now become the seat of the country's two highest courts, the *Bundesgerichts-hof*, the Federal Court of (ultimate) Appeal, and the *Bundesverfassungsgericht*, the Federal Constitutional Court, a post-war creation on the lines of the American Supreme Court, which has the last word on such matters as the interpretation of the constitution, the legality of political

Karlsruhe: The Case of Dr. Brach

movements and—a startling notion to us—the validity of acts passed by the parliament. Karlsruhe itself is quite a handsome town, of agreeable size (a quarter of a million), with a theatre, an opera house, amenities, a zoo. For some reason, possibly the total absence of medieval buildings, the Germans do not seem to like it, one seldom hears a good word for Karlsruhe. Norman Douglas, who lived there as a boy and went to the *Gymnasium*, was fond of it, and I rather agree with him.

On the pavement outside the *Landgericht*, there heaved a substantial queue, something one had believed to be more of a home speciality. Inside, the court was packed. A high criminal court was in session, a trial had just opened. In a hall of low-church bareness—no arms, no flag, no eagles, no emblem of any kind—a man stood by himself in front of the only row of empty seats, talking in a flat though fairly fluent voice. At a long table slightly raised, sat eight men and one woman in a row, the judges and the jury.

"I got as far as the entrance exam—well, and then I was called up—I was on the Russian front in '42. I was able to start again in 1945. I qualified four years later."

"Herr Doctor, and then you entered the Army Medical Corps at once?"

"Nearly at once. I was already married by then and, well, it was a particularly difficult time."

"Oh, quite. Please go on."

I was next to an obvious reporter. Witness? I managed to ask. He formed the words, *the accused*. And so it was. The man who stood talking almost casually without a warder or a guard, punctuated rather than examined by the bench, was the accused telling the story of his life to his judges as the first step of his trial for homicide.

He was a doctor in the German Army and he had shot a man in a public park who had exposed himself indecently to his small daughter. It was the trial of what was known as the Stabsarzt case, the case of the army doctor, and it had

85

rocked Germany for the last eight months. I had come in,
unwittingly, upon a *cause célèbre.*

The charge was neither manslaughter nor murder but—in
the nearest English approximation—wounding with intent
to do grievous bodily harm resulting in death [*Vorsätzliche
gefährliche Körperverletzung mit Todesfolge*], and this is the
story as it stood in common knowledge (through newspapers) before the trial. In the spring of 1958 a member of
the *Bundeswehr* Medical Corps, a Dr. Ulrich Brach, who had
so far been stationed at Karlsruhe, was transferred to an
Air-Arm station in the Northern Rhineland. Owing to
difficulties about living quarters there, his family, a wife and
child, had continued to live at their flat in Karlsruhe. Dr.
Brach went home to see them every other Saturday to Sunday,
driving a distance of some two hundred miles each way in
order to do so. In May of that year, his daughter was accosted
on her way to school by a man who exposed himself to her.
The girl told her mother, the mother went to the police;
no result. A few weeks later the same thing happened again.
Dr. Brach learned about it, but being away as he was throughout the week there was little he could do; except worry.
Meanwhile the man, always the same man according to the
girl, reappeared at intervals, and this went on for nearly three
quarters of a year. Then one winter day, the girl came running
in with a friend from school, " There's that man again," they
cried. It was a Saturday and Dr. Brach was at home. He acted
at once. The car was outside, he took the girls with him and
together they drove back the way they had just come. At the
edge of the city park, the daughter said, " That's him."
Dr. Brach stopped the car, told the girls to stay put, got out
and followed on foot. He overtook the man and told him that
he was arresting him and would now take him to the nearest
police station. The man appeared to acquiesce. The two
walked off. Then, somehow, the man managed to edge Dr.
Brach past a turning and they found themselves inside the
park. The doctor realised that this was not the proper way

and urged the man to follow *him*, but the man pressed on. It was just after half past one o'clock on a February afternoon, it was cold and the place was deserted. The man struck out for the centre of the park, the doctor walked beside him. Neither seems to have laid hands upon the other. They went on for some time, until at last the doctor saw a passer-by and called out to him. It turned out to be a lad of seventeen or sixteen. The boy came over and put himself on the man's other side. They set off, following a zig-zag course led by the man in the middle. The man was talking then. He said that he had been accused once before and they had believed the girl and he was fined ; he wouldn't have a chance this time. The doctor again urged him to come with them to the police. On they walked, the three of them, arguing as they went. Once the man broke into a trot, but the doctor and the boy caught up with him, and the doctor produced a pistol in a kind of demonstration and on they went. Presently they came to the end of the park.

To understand what followed one must know something of the particular topography of Karlsruhe. The town is one of those capitals that were started out of the blue on the inspiration of a prince. The Grand-Duke Karl had dreamed a dream when he had fallen asleep during a hunt. The hunt was taking place in a forest, and so in the middle of this forest the new capital was built. The time of the dream happened to be the eighteenth century, thus the inspiration was a singularly happy one—the architecture is charming and the town is still almost entirely circled by enormous woods. A part of them near the centre and the palace was tamed and trimmed into a park ; a short mile beyond, separated by a long high wall, lies the dense dark forest.

It was a portion of that wall which the boy, the doctor and the victim reached presently. The man asked if he might relieve himself. He stepped behind the wall, suddenly seized a branch of a nearby tree and began to pull himself up. The boy rushed at him, flung his arms about his legs and tried to drag him down; Dr. Brach whipped out his gun and fired two shots into the air. The boy ducked and sprang back. The man strained and struggled on, trying to get across the wall. Dr. Brach lowered his arm and as he did so a third shot went off, or was fired. It hit the man in the stomach and he slumped down. Dr. Brach administered first aid. Within a few minutes the man was dead.

He was later identified as an inhabitant of Karlsruhe, a man called Raimund Suk, a master-bookbinder by trade, married and fifty-one years old. One fine of a hundred marks [nine pounds ten] for indecent exposure was found recorded against him.

There were, locally and throughout Germany, two opposite reactions to these events, both expressed in letters—numbering many thousands—to the press, the police and the judiciary. One faction, many of which though by no means all were women and mothers, hailed the doctor as a hero. It should perhaps be said that there had been a wave of indecent exposures to children all over the country and that parents everywhere were much alarmed. The other side saw the doctor's action as an arbitrary exercise of self-justice, a defiance of democratic rule, a portent of renewed Army autocracy, and a sinister, possibly dangerous, reminder of the recent bad old days. It was pointed out that it was precisely as a member of the *Bundeswehr* that the doctor had been enabled to carry firearms, a permission otherwise not at all easily come by in postwar Germany.

For this, the packed court, the crowd outside.

" *Zur Sache.* Herr Doctor, will you now tell us something about the condition you were in that day? Mentally and physically . . . When did you get home? "

" It was just after 6 a.m."

" Having left your army station on Friday night? "

" Yes. I only came off duty at 9 p.m. Then I had to change out of uniform; I had something to eat; it was near to ten o'clock when I started."

Karlsruhe: The Case of Dr. Brach

" And then you drove all night ? What sort of a night was it ? " Note that this examination-in-chief is not made by counsel but by a judge.

" Conditions were quite bad."

" Ice ? "

" Oh, yes. And patches of fog on either side of Mannheim."

" Sounds filthy. We all know that road. Then, did you get some sleep ? "

" I lay down," said Dr. Brach in his flat, gloomy, almost lazy monotone.

The chief judge, the judge chairman or judge president as he is called, was a man in his fifties, fair, with a well-shaped head and features, a quick manner and a quick, urbane, intelligent voice that was manifestly upper-class. He appeared affable and at the same time quite penetrating. He and his two fellow judges wore simple black gowns trimmed with some plushy fur, white bow-ties and their own hair. The judge president alone had a black velvet biretta which he wore as he came in and then took off and placed in front of him. The judge on his right was a dark, bullet-headed man of about thirty-six or eight who talked with a broad Baden accent. The third judge was young, blond and thin, with gold-rimmed spectacles ; when he spoke, which was not often, it was in the High-German of the North and quite sharp. The six jurors had more of the individuality and self-possession one encounters in lay justices on the bench than in the men and women in the jury box ; and, in fact, they were sitting on the bench.

The prosecution was represented by the *Staatsanwalt*, an *Oberstaatsanwalt* in this case, who like the judges is a permanent civil servant and a lawyer who has passed two—pretty stiff—law examinations, but has not, and could never have, practised at the bar. On the Continent, bench and prosecution are two, usually distinct, civil service careers ; and in court, the public prosecutor sits alone in a kind of pulpit that is on the same level as, and only a foot or two from, the judges' table ;

whereas counsel for the defence, who is always a lawyer
(solicitor cum barrister) in private practice, has a seat on
ground-level near his client and is separated from the tribunal
and from his opponent, who is not his learned friend but
Herr Staatsanwalt to him, by the width of the whole floor.

" So that on the night before, you had had no sleep at all ? "
said the judge president.

" I may have dozed off," said Dr. Brach.

The accused doctor was a man just forty, tall, but of a
build that looked somehow both stiff and soft, the figure of
an indoor man. His face was on the heavy side, moony, with
small brown eyes and spectacles in some modern frame,
enough brown hair brushed back from a rising forehead and
a full weakish mouth ; and it gave nothing away. The
expression just missed sadness, and instead presented a curious
compound of hang-dog with stubbornness, smugness, sullen-
ness, self-control and calm which never changed. It was an
entirely unlit face, and during the whole of the trial it did not
once reflect an emotion of grief, sympathy or fear.

The crime he was charged with had taken place eight
months ago, and during the whole of that time the doctor
had not been in custody.

Presently he told the court how he had spent that morning,
catching up with his post, going through medical journals.
He was sitting in his study, it was past lunchtime, his daughter
was late from school (German children do go to school on
Saturday), he was getting rather annoyed. The girl came
rushing in, " Daddy, there's that man again ! "

" You knew at once what she meant ? "

" Oh, yes."

" What did you do ? "

" I dashed out to find him."

" Will you tell us what you did, exactly, step by step ? "

German judges have it all in front of them. They have had
weeks to go through it at home. They sit by no means every
day and the best of their working time is spent on paper work.

Karlsruhe: The Case of Dr. Brach

The accused may have been questioned—by another judge, the *Untersuchungsrichter* in the German-speaking countries, the *Juge d'instruction* in France—for a number of weeks or months. Everything he said has been taken down in writing, and this evidence, in a fat dossier lies open now at the relevant page before the presiding judge.

All the same, here too the evidence must be heard again at the trial, must be, as in English courts, oral and direct. [*Prinzip der Mündlichkeit und der Unmittelbarkeit.*] It all has to be said again for the last and final time that counts and, as in England, it will often turn out to be rather different from the original depositions.

" I quickly put on my overcoat and my shoes, I called out to my wife to telephone the police, I told the children to get into the car. On the way downstairs it occurred to me that if I did find him, it might be in the woods, so I ran back to get my revolver."

" Was it a loaded revolver ? "

" I only put the cartridges in on the stairs."

" What did you do with it then ? "

" I put it in my pocket."

" Dr. Brach—*what made you take a weapon ?* "

" I was perfectly clear in my mind that I had the right to prevent a possible escape."

They drove off. There followed some local directions. In a certain street not far from a park entrance, both children cried, " ' That's him, walking over there.' I pulled up, ordered the children to stay in the car, and ran after him——"

" One moment, Dr. Brach. How far was the man when you and the girls first caught sight of him ? "

" Oh, about fifty yards, sixty yards."

" Was he facing you ? "

" No. He was walking away very rapidly."

" So what the girls saw of him was his back ? "

" Yes, but they recognised him."

" Did they say how ? "

" I don't know, I didn't wait to hear, I didn't want him to get away."

" All you heard was, ' That's him ', and you were satisfied ? "

" They'd seen him before often enough."

" Dr. Brach, we know now that his name was Suk. Could you see, see from your car, what Herr Suk had on ? "

" He was wearing a dark-grey overcoat. It was a particularly long overcoat."

" And a hat."

" A hat."

" You caught up with him ? "

" I did. I arrested him."

" How did you do that ? "

" I put myself in front of him and I told him he was under arrest."

" Did you tell him why ? "

" No."

" *Did he ask you why ?* "

" No. I told him to follow me to the police station."

" What right did you think you had for doing that ? "

" Any citizen has the right to arrest an offender. I was taught that."

" Any citizen, Dr. Brach, has the right to arrest without judicial warrant *in flagrante delicto*, in the act, Dr. Brach, of committing an offence."

The doctor shrugged. " My girl was sure he was the man."

" And what did *he* do ? How did he react ? "

" He was quite meek. He seemed to follow me. I thought he realised. The moment I saw the type of man he was I knew that I wouldn't have to use the gun."

" What do you mean by that, Doctor ? "

" Oh, elderly. Quiet."

" Did you know then where you were going ? "

" Certainly. I meant to take him to the IVth precinct. The nearest."

" And yet you suddenly found yourself inside the park ? "

Karlsruhe: The Case of Dr. Brach

" Yes."

" How did that happen."

" I don't know."

" What did you do then ? "

" I told him it wasn't the right way and he just went on."

" And you let him ? "

" I told him he *must* come to the police with me."

" Herr Dr. Brach, Suk was a small man ? "

" Yes."

" Short and quite stout ? and in rather poor condition ? "

" Possibly."

" We know now that he was. At any rate, there was a man of five foot six and you are about six foot one and a good ten years younger—and it never occured to you to take him by the arm ? "

Dr. Brach did not answer. His face remained impenetrable. Then he went on in that level, dragging voice. " I kept hoping I would meet somebody, a policeman or some help. We were already beyond the palace and I could see there were people on the terrace, but it was too far to call. *He* just went on. I only had one thought in my mind : he mustn't get away, I mustn't let him escape. Then we met the boy. I asked him to come with me and help me to arrest this man."

" Did you tell him what for ? "

" I don't think so."

" And yet he agreed to come along with you ? "

" The man got excited and said I must send the boy away. He told me he knew all about this kind of thing and the police always believed the girl. He had been accused before and had had to pay a sum of money ; the police, he said, would never believe him now. I asked him to give me his name and address, and he would not. Then he suddenly ran away. It was only a few yards, we caught up with him at once. I thought I ought to warn him, so I showed him my revolver and he quietly walked on."

" Did you point it at him ? " asked the judge.

" No, I just showed it to him."

" How ? "

" On the flat of my hand."

" Do you consider that you threatened him ? "

" No. I only wanted him to know this was serious. I wanted to prevent him from trying to run away from me again."

" Did he comment on the weapon ? "

" No."

" Just walked on ? Docilely ? "

" Yes."

" Deeper into the park ? "

" Yes."

" Neither you nor the young man managed to march him, or attempted to march him round ? How long did this promenade continue ? "

" Twenty-five minutes, half an hour, perhaps longer."

They came to the wall. " He asked my permission to follow a call of nature, and I gave it."

" He asked *your* permission, Dr. Brach ? "

" Yes. Next thing I knew he was half in the tree and half on the wall and I thought : Oh my God, he's getting away, he's nearly across, and I fired two shots into the air to stop him. To my horror he didn't stop, the only thing left to do was to get him in the leg or foot so that he couldn't go on and escape, and I fired. He came down at once. I thought he must be wounded and went to him to give first aid, he died under my hands."

" We know now that he was shot in the heart through the stomach from a range of seven or eight feet—the medical and ballistics' gentlemen will tell us presently precisely how—will you tell us more about this third shot, Dr. Brach ? "

" Well, I must have aimed at his foot, there was one foot dangling, I only wanted to maim him so that he couldn't go on, I only wanted to wound him lightly in one of the extremities, I think my arm was down, the shot seemed to go off rather soon. . . ."

" Before you were able to take proper aim at, as you say, the foot ? "

" I don't know. It felt like it. I do not remember much between the first two shots and the third, I was in a state of great, of extreme nervous excitement, a state of shock . . . Everything seemed to go black. . . ."

" Dr. Brach, let us be quite clear about this. Did you intend to fire the third shot, or did it go off ? "

" I intended to fire if I had to, it may have gone off before I was ready. I'm not sure."

" Dr. Brach—when did you make up your mind to shoot at him, *before* the first two shots ? *Before* you saw Herr Suk was half across the wall ? Or afterwards, when according to you ' everything seemed to go black ' ? "

" I didn't think it would come to my having to shoot at him. Yes, perhaps I did decide before. I knew I had the right to shoot."

The judge president then touched upon a crucial point, the presence of the boy. " Didn't you see him, Doctor ? Didn't you realise he was there ? A few feet in front of you, hanging on to Suk's legs, making it presumably quite impossible for Suk to move—until you had scared him away with your warning shots—didn't you realise that he was in *your direct range* ? "

" I didn't see him. I was not aware of him at all."

" How can you explain that ? "

" I was in a state of shock."

" And yet a few minutes—seconds—later, as witnesses will tell us, you coolly and competently administered first aid ?"

" I was acting in my medical capacity then."

At this stage there were naturally a good many more questions to pinpoint the events ; the gist of the doctor's story, however, remained the same. It was a strange experience to hear this presentation of a case by both sides, as it were, in one ; not a prosecution case, followed by a defence case, but an attempt to build the whole case, the case as it might be presented in a summing-up, as it went. A strange experience to hear the (attenuated) inquisitorial procedure at work, to hear all questions, probing questions and soothing questions, accusatory and absolving questions, questions throwing a favourable light and questions having the opposite effect, flow from one and the same source, the bench, and only from the bench, while public prosecutor and counsel for the defence sat mute, taking notes.

" Dr. Brach, were you accustomed to handling a revolver ? "

" No. It was a new weapon. I had never used it before."

" You must have had some instruction or practice in the army ? "

" None at all. As a medical officer I had nothing to do with such things."

" You told us earlier today that you were called up and served during the war—before you were even a medical student—you must have had small-arms instruction then ? Didn't you know that a revolver is a most unreliable weapon—— ? "

" Yes, but——"

" Well, in heaven's name, man, didn't you know that it is about *the* most *uncertain, unsafe,* weapon there is ? " This was said with considerable severity, although not so much in the manner of a judge addressing an exhortation to the dock, as in the tone of man to man.

" When it comes to one's child being indecently molested twice a week——"

" Twice a week ? This is the first time you told this court anything of the kind ! "

" It happened all the time."

" You did not give that figure, or anything like it to the examining judge ? "

(It had already come out that the doctor had said very little during the preliminary investigation; instead he had given a detailed interview to an illustrated weekly. " Why did you do that ? " " I don't know." " Don't you know the motives for your actions, Dr. Brach ? " " Well, the editor had asked me to.")

" My wife went to the police," said Dr. Brach.

" How often ? Twice a week ? "

" Again and again. It didn't do any good."

" *Herr Oberstaatsanwalt,* have you any information about such complaints ? " The prosecutor answered that his department knew only of the one that had been lodged in the spring of 1958.

" My wife went at least a dozen times," said Dr. Brach, " and she didn't go every time it happened."

" And these alleged visitations always took place in the park ? "

" Yes, on the girl's way to school."

" Couldn't she have taken another way ? " asked the younger judge.

" She could have gone through the town," said the judge president, " by making a slight detour she need not have gone through the park at all."

" Yes, she could have."

" Did you not tell her ? "

" I think I did. I know my wife told her."

The younger judge, the one who spoke with the Baden accent, said, " You *think* you told her ? Didn't you say, ' Look here, you mustn't go to school through the park, I forbid you to go to school through the park ' ? "

" I did speak to her," Dr. Brach said, deadpan and helpless.

" One or two more points. Can you tell us something more about your state of mind on that Saturday noon, Doctor ? You hadn't slept, luncheon was late, you were pretty irritable ? When your girl came in with the news, did you feel annoyed at your week-end being spoilt ? "

" That didn't occur to me," said Dr. Brach. (This question of the judge was later harshly criticised in the press as frivolous.)

At that point a jolly blare drowned all other sound in court. A troop of *Bundeswehr* with brass band was marching by in the street below. " Are they serenading you, Dr. Brach ? " asked the judge, whereupon court and public broke into a common gust of good-natured laughter. Dr. Brach cracked an uneasy smile.

" To wind up, we should like to know something about your general attitude, your *Lebensauffassung*. How do you personally feel about the phenomenom of exhibitionism ? Do you think exhibitionists are people who act under a pathological compulsion ? Do you think they are sick people ? or perverts ? Are they particularly repulsive to you ? "

" I think an adult who exposes himself indecently to a child is a criminal."

" Now is that your attitude as a man and a father, or is it also your attitude as a physician ? "

" I cannot understand it at all. As a sane human being I just cannot enter the psyche of such a creature."

The examination of the accused was over and the witnesses were called in. All the witnesses. Men, women and girls, a gaggle of about fifteen, stood uncertainly about the floor. The judge president waved them to come forward, then himself gave them a little formal, but not perfunctory, speech. Their responsibility here, he said, was a grave one. They *knew* that they must speak the truth ? They must neither depart from it through malice, through favour nor through fear, and if they did not remember or were not certain, they must say so. The truth was essential here, for the accused, for the course of justice ; for themselves. Any one of them *might* be put on oath, and telling a lie on oath was perjury and the penalty hard labour. And even if they were not put on oath, they were still under the same absolute obligation to speak the truth, and could be imprisoned for bearing false witness. Even to tell an untruth by carelessness or mistake was punishable. " You have understood me ? You are quite clear about this in your minds ? "

The witnesses nodded. " Very well then." And they all trooped out again. " I should like to take the children first and then the *Herren Experten*, but before them I must take young Schmitt because he is in the middle of an exam."

Young Schmitt, a pastry-cook apprentice, standing six foot five, was fetched back and took the floor. There is no such thing as a witness box. After a brisk formula—you are neither related nor connected with the accused, nor his employer, nor in his employment ?—they went *in medias res*.

" The doctor called for your help ? Whereabouts was that ?"

" In the Rose Garden, near the Romeo and Francesca Monument." This union of Shakespeare with Dante, caused great unsuppressed joy to all educated Germans present.

" He called for your help, and you complied ? "

" Yes."

" What did you think it was all about ? "

" I didn't know at first," said the boy.

" Yet you were ready to help ? One stranger against another ? "

" Well, the doctor had said something about an arrest."

" And you took his word ? "

" . . . Yes."

" Why ? "

" I don't know . . . The look of it . . . I think I understood quite soon that it was about some indecent assault. When I heard them talking to each other I became certain that the man had raped the doctor's daughter."

" Was that what you thought ? What impression did they give you ? "

" Very calm, both of them. Just talking, and walking on. Then the man tried to run away, that was nothing. Just a few yards and he was puffing. He was an old little man, and was wearing such a heavy overcoat, he couldn't have got away."

" What about the wall ? "

" He was quick enough there. I wouldn't have thought he had it in him. He must have known the place well. There's no other place with that sort of tree along the whole of that wall."

" So in your opinion he could have got away ? "

" Oh no," said the boy. " As soon as I saw what he was up to I got hold of his legs. I was holding him easily, he didn't have a chance."

" Well, you *are* quite a young giant," said the judge. " What happened next ? "

" I was just about to get him down when I heard Dr. Brach shout, ' Stay put ! '——"

" Addressed to you ? Or to Herr Suk ? "

" I don't know. I suppose I thought he meant Suk."

" Dr. Brach, do you remember shouting that ? "

The doctor still sat from where he had spoken last, alone, unguarded, in a row of open seats. He said, " I cannot remember, but I may have."

" Then shots—crashing near me—I jumped. The last one must have nearly got me."

" And then ? "

" Suk was lying on the ground and the doctor was kneeling over him. Suk was speaking, I could clearly hear the words, he said, ' Oh, how mean you are.' *Oh wie gemein sind sie.* Then he died. I didn't realise it at the time, but he must have died."

" Dr. Brach——? "

" I did not hear it."

" I said to the doctor, ' For God's sake, what did you do ? what did you shoot with ? ' He said, ' With my revolver, of course.' *Selbstverständlich.* I had the impression that he was quite sure of himself, I mean he gave the impression of having acted absolutely legally. I ran to get help, I had to run half a mile till I saw two policemen near the palace."

" Gentlemen of the jury—any questions ?

" *Herr Oberstaatsanwalt*—any questions ? "

" Yes. —Herr Witness, you said you were just about to get him down ? Did you mean by this that you were able to prevent the victim from getting across the wall ? "

" I was."

" In fact, you were master of the situation ? "

" Oh, yes."

" You were at that moment effectively able to prevent an escape ? "

" Certainly."

" Thank you."

" *Herr Verteidiger*—any questions ? "

Counsel for the defence (long black gown, untrimmed ; white knitted tie), rose for the first time. He was a fair, rather lounging, young man, the son, one heard, of a trial lawyer famed for his oratory. " Dr. Brach gave you the impression of a man who had acted absolutely within his rights, who had acted legally ? "

" *He* seemed to have no doubt about it," said the boy.

" Dr. Brach—any question to the witness ? "

" No, thank you."

After eleven, there was a brief adjournment. In a narrow ante-room, where the press left their overcoats, journalists and lawyers stood about eating sandwiches out of their briefbags in a great buzz of voices. Judges and prosecutor passed through freely. Dr. Brach stood in the doorway with his counsel. The populace, a crowd as large as could squeeze in, remained in their roped-off half of the court, guarded by two members of the Baden State Police, side-arms in belts.

After the adjournment came the children's evidence, always a disagreeable experience, here remarkable chiefly for the

Germany

way in which the judges handled it. Child witnesses everywhere nowadays are examined with great consideration, sometimes with attempts at delicacy that are bound to misfire in the circumstances. In England one often sees a lady barrister chosen by the Crown (children by the nature of these cases are practically always prosecution witnesses), " And now, Rosemary, will you tell his Lordship——? And you will remember, won't you, to keep your voice up, to speak just a teeny bit louder ? " The job, getting a child to tell what really happened, dulcet approach or not, is a fearfully difficult one, if not hopeless ; sweet Portia and the sympathetic policeman and his Lordship are simply not in the same world with little Rosemary in the box, fluffed up by her mother for the day. It has been put down for ever by Mr. Richard Hughes in *A High Wind in Jamaica.*

The doctor's girl was sent in. Girls of twelve can look almost anything, this one was just a nice child. " Come up, my dear," said the judge president ; " up here, come to me." Up on the dais she went, round the judges' table, to his chair. He turned sideways to face her, and asked her name. The child sketched a curtsy. He asked her some questions about school ; he nearly made her laugh ; then, friendly and matter of fact, he told her that now they must speak about those disagreeable things. He and the younger judge asked all that had to be made known or clear. Where they could, they were off-hand ; they minced no words where words could not be minced. The jury heard all the precise evidence. His voice, though distinct enough, stayed private, and by keeping the girl turned to him, he never allowed her to become quite aware of her surroundings. Once the prosecutor rose to submit exclusion of the public on grounds of decency, but the judge president turned it down. Once the public guffawed and he silenced it with a rebuke as sharp as the guillotine. The girl, throughout, sounded cheerful and detached.

It was well done. Almost anyone else in the judges' position would have attempted to do the same—although perhaps not with quite that degree of informality—but it might not have come off. Those two men had the touch that cannot be learnt. Perhaps the secret of it was the lack of sentimentality and condescension ; there was nothing false about their manner, it seemed informed by moderation, good sense and a respect for other people's feelings. I should perhaps say that it was a performance of high human quality and that a German court of law was the last place where I should have dreamt to encounter it. (Perhaps I should also say that I had not put a foot inside Germany for nearly thirty years and that I had decided never to enter it again as long as I lived ; unless it were to do a job.)

The substance of the girl's evidence was that there had been indecent exposure, but no attempt at assault, by the same man, " He always wore the same grey overcoat "—" Yes, in summer, too "—on the same way through the park. Sometimes she had been alone and sometimes she had been with her friend and it had happened [unhesitating answer] twenty times. Mama had gone to the police ; a lady from the police had called at home ; how often ? perhaps three times. And why had they kept on going to school by that way ? Well, sometimes they hadn't, but then it was much nearer and the school forbade girls to walk home through the town. Then had not the school been told ? Oh, no.

The second girl—not quite such a child—was called and her evidence was much the same. " Twenty times." Then came the experts—Walther 6.76—abdominal cavity—tidying up facts that had been loosely known. Then the park witnesses, the people who had heard the shots and hurried to the scene. These shed no new light ; indeed some of them seemed still to be animated by some wild surmise.

" . . . .Oh dear, I said to myself, there is another of those suicides, and sure enough, under the bushes there was the poor suicide lying on the ground and the accused gentleman here was bending over him ; I said to the accused gentleman, excuse me, sir, do you know the suicide? Were you trying to prevent him? There are so many suicides in this place, but he didn't answer me, he didn't say anything, he only looked at the suicide."

"Dr. Brach, do you remember hearing this lady address you?"

No, said Dr. Brach.

"So I asked him again, I asked the gentleman if he was so upset because he had tried to prevent the poor suicide——"

"He was *upset*?"

"I was sure he was so upset because he hadn't been able to prevent the poor suicide."

Before adjourning the judge asked the public prosecutor for a complete check of complaints received by the police from Mrs. Brach between May 1958 and February 1959. The prosecutor replied that he would arrange for an immediate examination of the files and hoped to be able to make the results available to the court by to-morrow morning.

It may seem surprising that such a matter should have been left unexplored until this last hour. It is something that happens all the time. Facts come out at the trial which the layman at least thinks vital to the issue and nobody, one finds, has so far thought or wished or bothered to follow them up. Here, moreover, there had been eight months of investigation.

The judge then ordered a local reconstruction to be held that afternoon. "We shall meet here, gentlemen, at a quarter to three. We shall want the gentlemen of the jury; the *Herr Staatsanwalt*; Herr Dr. Brach—naturally; the *Herren Professoren*; and we want young Schmitt, and [looking at them] such gentlemen of the press as wish to attend. At a quarter to three then, gentlemen. The hearing is suspended."

———————————————

We set out in the October sunshine, the court (unrobed) with

Karlsruhe: The Case of Dr. Brach

the jury in front, the rest of us following pell-mell. The judge president was dressed in a well-made not very new suit and the same kind of shoes. No hat. Dr. Brach had put on a mackintosh, his lawyer a semi-sports jacket. There were perhaps ten reporters and a modest assortment of portable cameras. Our crocodile was flanked by some Baden Police whose function it was to stop the traffic at our crossings and to dissuade members of the public from attaching themselves to us.

When we came to the park entrance, we stopped and Dr. Brach marked the position from which he first saw Suk. The doctor moved about, co-operative enough, but in the same dulled impenetrable manner he had shown in court. The more one saw of him the harder it became not only to interpret his emotions and reflections, but to place him. Certainly not a young man, nor yet quite middle-aged; not a particularly German face, nor for that matter a Central European or a Latin or an American face, but rather a generic contemporary face, the face of a middling professional man or business executive anywhere. One could have met him at a Rotary luncheon in Michigan or in South America, or in the surgery of a Midland town G.P. He could have been a member of a Russian delegation. A middle-flight, white, plastic-age man.

We entered the park. Dr. Brach was to lead the way. First we took one path, then another. Once we missed a turning and came to a massed halt. Autumn leaves were on the trees and the landmarks must have looked quite different. One wondered : had he been back since then ? The slanting sun lay on the lawns and warm on our shoulders, the trees were tall and old, the ground springy with moss. The experts congratulated each other on their outing. Couples passed us, and children with hoops. Many of us that afternoon must have felt that to be alive was best. I happened to walk next to the psychiatric professor from Heidelberg. He talked about the Podola case. He had been impressed by Podola's reactions on being shown his own diary in the witness-box, and by what the medical expert—was it a Dr. Ashby?—had said about it afterwards. He said we were quick to hang. I said that we were indeed.

Presently we came to the sculpture of a pastoral couple, young Schmitt entered the picture and stepped to the doctor's side. People turned their heads as we passed by, but most of those who wished to join us believed us to be a film company. In a clearing we saw some red squirrels chasing acorns. Hither and fro—it was a long walk and the longer it went on the odder it appeared and there grew a thick sense of unspoken comment. At last we came to the wall. There it was, as one had heard, with the low-forked tree beside it : in the shade, a little dank, looking, as such places do to the beholder, non-committal, innocent.

We drew up in a half-circle and, directed by the judge and a measurements' man, they re-enacted the scene. You stood here—you there—one more step to the right if you please— Herr Doctor, will you take the pistol—lift your arm ? A law undergraduate was asked to take the dead man's part, swung himself on the wall—" Not as easy as it looks," he called— young Schmitt sprang forward—the doctor took two steps— cameras clicked, someone stood by the bushes with a clip-board taking a shorthand note.

———————————

We returned in the dusk by a straight route. Five minutes for judges and counsel to robe and the hearing was continued. The judge president said that they hoped to be able to finish with the witnesses this evening so as to have a clear day to-morrow for the psychiatric evidence and the closing speeches.

The doctor's wife chose to give evidence. She conveyed at last a coherent picture of the strain the family had lived under during that preceding year. Her husband, absent for twelve days out of every fourteen, had been growing desperate under the sense of being unable to look after them. They had tried with no success to find a place to live in nearer to his post. The girl, she estimated, must have been molested some fifteen times in all. In February, she herself had been eight months gone with their second child.

She spoke looking at the judge, every now and then she turned towards her husband. He did not look at her ; he never met her eye.

Of course she had been to the police . . . Not every time, how could she ? What with everything, and they had no help at home ; besides, she had felt that it was so very bad for the child : the questioning, every time. The child thank God had not seemed to be much disturbed, one had to be grateful for that, though her husband said one could not tell, about later on, about after-effects. Oh, he was so worried ! Then, on that last day, the child had come home in such a state—beside herself—never, never had she seen the child like that before. " It frightened us."

Next came a woman, housewife, fifty-some years old, who claimed that she also had been indecently molested in the park by the same man. It had been a very shocking experience to her, it had upset her so much that she had been nervously ill—as her doctor could certify—for some time afterwards. She had been to the police at the time.

How did she come to identify that man with the late Herr Suk ?

As it happened, only a week or two after the incident she had seen him walking in the street past her own window. She had called her husband, " Look, *da geht das Schwein*." He had worn an ordinary suit and jacket whereas in the park he had been wearing a long grey overcoat which he opened when he saw her. After that she had watched out and seen the man several times again, always in the suit during working hours and in that overcoat at midday and the evening.

" Did you ever find out his name ? "

Not then. But after the murder— I mean after the Herr
Doctor— She had been shown photographs of the dead man
and she was positive, quite positive.

A young girl, a typist of nineteen, gave evidence of the same
experience. No, she hadn't thought much about it; she had
looked away and put it out of her mind. No, not to the police.
Then she saw the picture in an illustrated paper. There could
be no mistake. The overcoat. "It was a quite unusual overcoat; old-fashioned."

Next came a forester. He declared that while his department
had been receiving constant complaints of exhibitionist
activities in the state forests, the complaints had ceased over-
night after the 14th of February.

"To what cause do you ascribe this fact?"

"Mainly, I suppose, to the police patrols that were sent
after that date."

Then there came some evidence as to character. A letter
by the chief of the doctor's Army Group was read. As a
medical officer, the major general wrote, Dr. Brach was
technically competent enough "but lacking in human qualities.
Sympathy and understanding are absent or underdeveloped."
The head of the hospital where the doctor had served as
intern for a number of years had come in person to testify in
stolid tones to his uprightness and decency. "He was the
most right-thinking assistant I have ever had."

"In view of the letter we have just heard," said the judge,
"might there be, in your opinion, some discrepancy between
his professional and his human qualities?"

"None whatsoever."

And finally the witnesses were called back again *en masse*.
They stood, facing the bench; the judge president rose,
covered himself with the black biretta and administered the
oath. "Will you lift your right hand and repeat after me, one
by one, 'I swear it as truly as God may help me.'" The whole
court stood, and it was very slow and solemn. After that we
adjourned to 8.45 on the next morning. It was then half past

Karlsruhe: The Case of Dr. Brach

seven p.m. How right they had been about continental hours.

———————

The psychiatric estimate, delivered by the Heidelberg Professor of Forensic Medicine, a psycho-medical lecture citing Freud, Krafft-Ebbing, lesser household names, Jung, the works—how would it have fallen on English judicial ears ? How for that matter did it fall on German ones. For the jurors and the bench sat through the disquisition with the kind of blank attentiveness one so often sees on jury's faces. The professor began by describing the phenomenon of exhibitionism, the one, the only one, of all the sexual aberrations that was turned entirely against its object, hostile, destructive, isolating, *anti* : anti-union, anti-communication, anti-love. The impulse of the man who exposed himself to women and female children was hatred, what he sought to inspire was humiliation, disgust or fear. Most authorities now held that the effect of such an experience on children and young girls could be an extremely grave one, resulting in frigidity and other deep, often life-long, disturbances. All of that, the professor said, must have been particularly well-known to Dr. Brach. He, it must be remembered, qualified at a time—after the end of the Hitler régime and its ban on Freud and all his ideas—when German medical teaching was flooded once more with psycho-analytical literature. A man taking his degree in those post-war years could not have failed to have been impressed by these theories.

As for Dr. Brach himself, the professor had interviewed and examined him ; he would describe him as a man rather lacking in initiative, decent, but clumsy and without drive, a man who found it very hard indeed to get a grip on reality. "I should call him an excellent 'second' and a very poor 'first'. In other words, he has to be led. It is not surprising that he made a good assistant, but failed when he had to act on his own. He is a man totally devoid of any personal aggressiveness, and it is just this which made him act in the way he did act when he had to cope with the situation in the park. Of course he chose a fantastically roundabout and inadequate way of dealing with that situation, but looking at it from a subjective point of view, it would be right to say that *he* saw the shooting as the only means open to him."

There was no question of premeditation. There could also be no question, the professor concluded, of diminished responsibility within the meaning of Paragraph 51, Subsection 1 and 2 of the law.

" The court is very much obliged to you, Herr Professor," said the judge. " I don't think we need to take your oath? I understand that you are under permanent oath? "

" I am, sir."

The prosecution announced that they had now succeeded in checking those complaints, a representative of the police was here and ready to take the stand. It turned out that the doctor's wife had been to the police six times in all, the last time about one week before the events in February. " Fair enough," said the reporters.

" The evidence [*Beweisaufnahme*] is now closed," said the judge. And this was the end of the first stage of the trial.

" *Herr Staatsanwalt* if you please——"

The public prosecutor rose in his pulpit, a long, gaunt man, a local also by his accent. So far his role had been confined to a few questions and one or two—unsuccessful—attempts to close court. (Exclusion of the public, which is ordered at the judge's discretion in cases liable to affect public decency, and by prescription in all cases of divorce, is a serious matter here as it means the exclusion of the press as well. The press is not merely forbidden to report on certain matters, it is forbidden to be there at all. The court sits and hears alone.)

The prosecutor began straightaway by stating that he was satisfied that there was no evidence of any intent to kill. Then, in a long-winded, lifeless speech, he went through the factual evidence in a review that was more in the nature of a judicial summing up than a presentation of a prosecution case.

The *Staatsanwalt* is supposed to stand as an attorney for the public interest. The term, though habitually translated as Public Prosecutor, means literally State Attorney, the word prosecutor is not in it, and the office itself was first introduced —against much resistance—in 1849 in Prussia as a measure of liberal reform. And it is the duty of the *Staatsanwalt*, just as it is the duty of the prosecution in England to-day, to present the true facts of a case rather than press for a conviction *per se*.

Coming to the position in law, the prosecutor said, it was true that under Paragraph 127 of the Code of Criminal Procedure any citizen had the right to arrest an offender caught red-handed. The pursuit of the deceased *might* fall within the meaning of ' caught red-handed ', and Dr. Brach by inviting the deceased to follow him to a police station could be said to have acted within that law. But there was a limitation : the law did not admit of any physical violence used or harm inflicted in such an arrest or pursuit. Therefore the third shot fired by Dr. Brach, a shot fired with the intention to wound, was not justified under that law. " It must be admitted that at the time the accused had been under considerable psychological strain, and there can be no doubt that he has acted while under the influence of great excitement, but this does not absolve him of his responsibility for his own wilful decision to wound another man, nor of the charge of carelessness. I therefore submit that Dr. Brach be found guilty of intent to do grievous bodily harm resulting in death." As to sentence, the prosecution would submit that the penalty should be severe enough to make it clear to the accused and clear, above all, to the public that such a course of action was intolerable, " Or we shall be in danger of seeing the course of justice defeated in the chaos of self-justice ! "

It is the rule for the prosecution, and defence, to end their pleadings with an exact submission as to sentence, and this was now awaited with considerable suspense.

"In mitigation, we have Dr. Brach's impeccable record—*Vorleben*—there are no previous convictions whatsoever. We shall have to remember the fact that, whatever the outcome of this trial, he will still have to face on the one hand a hearing before a disciplinary tribunal of the army, and on the other a claim of compensation in the civil courts by the widow of the deceased." One would also have to consider the army regulation under which any member of the forces sentenced to one year or more of prison was automatically dismissed the service. Dr. Brach, at present, was still carrying on his duties in the Medical Corps. "I therefore submit to the Venerable Court that a sentence of ten months would be the just and sufficient retribution in this case."

There was a slight stir. Leave to speak was then given to the lawyer representing the victim's widow, counsel for, as it is called, the co-ordinated prosecution [*Nebenklage*], who said in a few words that he concurred with the views expressed by the public prosecutor; it was not his mandate to seek retributary punishment and he was prepared to second the submission. And this brought the court to the morning break.

There were a number of young people present that morning, law students, and discussion waxed high. "The prosecution as good as asked them to save the doctor's army career—he's fixed the sentence so that the doctor can stay on . . ." But when one tried to find out if and how much this shocked them, they became unsure: Yes perhaps, or not at all; it was only the surprise. The populace was openly anti-Brach. "He's not a man," was most often heard. "Why didn't he knock the old fellow down?" A beerhouse keeper was holding forth, "D'you want to know *my* sentence? I'd send him to the front, front-line in the next war. Africa or somewhere . . ." I say populace, because that is what they were, with a fine streak of *tricoteuses* among them. Here, too, there seems to operate that unwritten rule that the law-courts are public to one kind of public, while the other half stays away unless it can get admission into the better half of court. Only very innocent American ladies brave the public gallery at the Old Bailey. It is not a good way, because it keeps good people out; and it will go on as long as the public, instead of being made honourably welcome, are herded, squeezed and segregated in a remote, or materially or symbolically inferior portion of the court. Our own queueing system, by which people cannot get in again after the luncheon adjournment because the afternoon queue has already formed some hours earlier, makes it impossible for any member of the public ever to see the whole of a trial of any length or interest. Small wonder then that only those go, who only go in the hope of hitting on some dramatic hour. If you treat people like a crowd lined up outside a freak-show, that is the kind of crowd you'll get.

" The court gives leave to speak to the gentleman for the defence."

" Most Venerable Court——"

Perhaps the most consistent feature of this trial so far had been moderation, the climate of impartial reserve, the abstention from censorious comment: censure of the dead man against whom nothing could be said to have been proved, restraint from censure (on the whole) of Dr. Brach who was not yet convicted. The faintly loutish young lawyer, who had sprawled through most of the case, took at once to the wings of rhetoric. Striding the floor and flapping the sleeves of his gown, he got off on a sustained *vibrato*.

" The true accused, Most Venerable Court, the true accused does not stand before you to-day, the true accused has escaped the arm of temporal justice. And it may well be that it is this shot, this shot fired by Dr. Brach, which has made it impossible for us to hear one day the dire news of a child murdered in the woods of Karlsruhe. . . ." His case, when he came down to it, ran to this. His client had never had the slightest intention of exercising self-justice, his one, his almost obsessive aim throughout had been to deliver up that man to the lawful representatives of justice. When finally the offender attempted to escape across the wall, the doctor had been drawn into what in law constituted an emergency situation, a *Notstand* or *Notwehrlage*, a situation in which he was justified to shoot as a matter of public duty, just as he would have been justified to shoot in self-defence. The emergency situation here had been created by the danger threatening the community if the offender had managed to escape and remain at large. The law recognised such emergencies.

The young lawyer had done his homework. He cited a string of decisions. The High Court of Appeal at Leipzig in 192— acquitting a pair of gendarmes for shooting down a known fruit thief in flight, a watchman opening fire on a burglar on the roofs, a detective exonerated for doing so on a criminal resisting arrest. . . . Then he returned to the more emotional appeal. The speech went on for an hour and a half. Most closing speeches are too long, or too long for their burden. An odd professional blind-spot, as it must be obvious that these pleadings would more persuas-ive—which is their explicit aim—if they did not weary, bore and, as the quarter hours go ticking by, reduce to numb despair the captive listeners whom they are intended to persuade.

Crescendo upon crescendo, it went on like a symphony that cannot end. " The case of Dr. Brach is the tragedy of an honest man, decency, morality and the law acquit this man." Counsel stood still and faced the jurors, " *You* judge in the name of the people, and the people acquit this man. If you convict him you will have convicted yourselves ! And the people——"

" Objection ! "

Axed by the judge, the young man stopped in his tracks.

Karlsruhe: The Case of Dr. Brach

"You know that this is tantamount to intimidation of the jury."

Deflated, off-balance, the defence ended on a single sentence. "In the name of the people, I ask you to return a verdict of Not Guilty."

The prosecutor now has the right to reply. He did so. He made two points. One, the decisions cited did not, in his opinion, apply here as those various defendants had all been members of police or auxiliary security forces exercising their official duties. Two, there could be no question in this case of an emergency situation as it was understood by the law, the situation here had been created by the weakness and indecision of Dr. Brach, and the legally indispensable element of necessity was lacking as there had been in fact another way out, which Dr. Brach, contrary to his duty under the law, had failed to ascertain. Thus the prosecution must adhere to its original submissions. An acquittal would open the fatal path of self-justice.

Dr. Brach was told that he had the last word. He looked at a loss.

"You concur with the submission of your defence counsel?" said the president.

"I concur with the submission of my defence counsel."

There is no form of summing-up. Judge and jury withdrew at once to consider their verdict.

It was about two o'clock and everybody else, staff, public, press, and Dr. Brach, went home or about their business. To avoid a general hanging about it is customary here for the judge to give a time before which the court will not return in any circumstances. In this case the hour given was 6 p.m.

It is now time to say a word about the jury. The jury, we have seen, retired with the bench. I have been calling them the jurors and the jury, and the trial a jury trial, because that seemed the simplest way of saying *Schöffen* and *Geschworene* and *das Schwurgericht*, but the jury as we know it does no longer exist in Germany. They did have an equivalent, or near equivalent: our model as adopted by France and introduced here under French influence in the nineteenth century. Twelve men or (later) women. Selected more or less at random. Sitting apart; deliberating in secret, alone. Sole judges of fact. Not judges of law. Sole judges of innocence or guilt. Final judges of innocence, irreversible in acquittal. But this system was abolished, not by whom we might think but by the Weimar Republic. One of the reasons given for the abolition throws a curious sidelight. The juries were not good at weighing evidence fairly. There were, in the opinion of the courts, too many convictions. The people left on their own proved to be more severe, illiberal and prejudiced than the jurists.

The present form, the *Schöffen-* or *Schwurgericht*, is a hybrid form of jury trial and it differs from ours in almost every respect. (One might call the *Schöffen* lay justices or assessors rather than jurymen, but this while more accurate in some ways would be misleading again in others.) German jurymen are not selected at random. They are taken, by lot, from a local list made up of substantial citizens and representative citizens, men and women of good repute, men of political deserts and the like, and empanelled for a term of one year, or in the more busy jurisdictions for one session. M.D.s and teachers are not automatically exempt, and in fact the people who can get most easily excused from jury duty are housewives and nursing mothers.

The number of the jury is not twelve. It varies according to offence and court between two, three or six.

The jury does not sit apart. It sits on the bench with the judge or judges, much in the manner of the lay justices sitting with a qualified chairman at English Quarter Sessions. Two jurors with one judge, or three jurors with two judges in the lower criminal courts; two with three in the higher courts, except in capital cases where there must be a jury of six sitting with three judges. (Civil courts in Germany do not sit with juries.)

Karlsruhe: The Case of Dr. Brach

The jury does not deliberate alone, and it is not the sole judge of innocence or guilt. The verdict is between the jury and the bench, and it is arrived at not by unanimity but by majority. Plain absolute majority—one man, one vote; the presiding judge does not have a casting vote, and there cannot be a tied jury as their number is uneven in all compositions. $2 + 1 = 3$; $3 + 2 = 5$; $6 + 3 = 9$.

The jurors *are* judges of law in so far as they decide not only on the verdict, but on sentence also; and on this they vote again on equal terms with the professionals. They *must* give their reason why; they cannot leave it at the single word spoken by their foreman and keep mum for the rest of their natural lives. And lastly they are not the final judges of innocence : a verdict of acquittal is reversible, as the prosecution can appeal, and appeals are decided by judges only.

What is our first reaction to such a system? Shock perhaps of judges talking cheek by jowl to juries. The big question of course is that of independence. In England juries are regarded sacrosanct; but sacrosanct somewhat in the manner of a temple sacrifice, the judge is the high priest, they the caged birds of omen. Placed as they are in Germany " up there ", treated to the deference, sharing pen and paper, elbow-room, the amenities of the court, closeted with the court, can these risen laymen, these temporary officers of the law, resist the judicial embrace? Will they, can they, do they, stand up in what is not the jury-room but the counsel chamber?

One has got to think of the particular composition of the jury here, with its high leaven of professional men, foremen, social workers, people not unversed in negotiation or in public duty. Nor is the gap in status what it would be in England; the judicature on the Continent is an honourable and esteemed career, not far below that of a university professor, but it does not bestow on the incumbent anything like the power, the awe and the general sense of elevation that surround an English judge. Thus a German juryman should feel no more at a sensible disadvantage arguing with a German judge than, say, a member of the House of Commons would feel in dealing with a senior civil servant very much at home in his own department. And above all there are safeguards of procedure. It is known what goes on, or should go on, behind the closed doors. Bench and jury, like committees, follow certain rules, and these rules are laid down by law. A junior judge must speak first, resuming the facts of the case and covering points of law. After him the jurors speak one by one, giving their opinions with their reasons ; the judge president speaks last. The order of voting is, jurors first, after them the most junior judge and so on. The judge president, the man who dominated the trial, votes last.

How far are these rules observed ? There seems to be a consensus among lawyers that they are. At any rate there is nothing in the way of contempt of court to prevent a juryman from making public any breach that may have occurred ; on the other hand the public is probably less vigilant and concerned about the matter than it would be here.

The Karlsruhe Law-courts are housed in a rambling building, one wing modernised the other not, in a tree-lined avenue near the palace. Away from Staircase D and the lingerers of the Brach case, all lay calm. The hum, such as it was, might have been that of a hospital. I spent the afternoon trying to find my bearings in the neat bright corridors, studying the name cards on the painted double doors.

LANDGERICHTSRAT C.   Dɾ. WOLFRAM SCH.

DR. JUR. STOLZ INQUISITIONS
2—4 p.m. except Wednesday

DR. ANNA K. JUGENDBERATUNGSTELLE
If No Answer Please Try Room 204

Karlsruhe: The Case of Dr. Brach

AMMELDEZIMMER: DO NOT KNOCK

BERATUNGSZIMMER IVTE KAMMER

SITZUNGSZIMMER

Opening the right padded door there would be a court
in session, room-sized, light-furnished, very clean, nearly
empty, with a single judge holding a subdued, soft-voiced
colloquy with a defendant. No policeman, no uniform in
sight.

"May I have your *personalia*?"

". . . .Thirty-two. Principal cashier."

"Previous convictions?"

"None at all."

"Encouraging. Now what about those eight hundred
marks—is that true?"

"Unfortunately true."

"And the three hundred and fifty the month after?"

"All of it."

"Now what started your difficulties? You had rather a
good salary. Any extraordinary expenditure?"

"Well, there was my being engaged . . ."

"Presents?"

"Presents, too. Taking her out . . . We used to go for
week-end trips. Ski-ing in the Black Forest, that meant two
outfits."

"Night clubs?"

"Ah, yes."

"Expensive night clubs?"

"I'm afraid so."

"Which ones?"

"The Green Monkey."

"Hmn, yes—there *are* even more expensive ones in
Karlsruhe," said the judge.

It was a quiet day—defalcation—an elderly man charged
with dangerous driving of his Volkswagen—a divorce,

" Sorry, but you can't come in here "—an insurance fraud—
and the hearings were not seamless, number nine, here, does
not tread on number eight sir, but " Do we have anything
on at four o'clock ? "

" Not till 4.15, *Herr Amtsgerichtsrat*," says the clerk. For
parties and witnesses are summoned to the fixed times at
which the court is reasonably certain to be able to hear them.
" It was thought, sir, that Phoenix-Life might turn out on the
longish side."

" Oh, quite. The 4.15 lot haven't arrived yet by any
chance ? "

" No, sir."

" Ah, well . . ." The judge gets up, gathering his dossiers.
The public prosecutor stays behind and lights a cigarette.
He comes over; names himself. " Was it interesting ?
Were you able to follow ? Can I help you ? "

Keeping on the move, clock in mind, I managed to take in
a short case here and there and sit through stretches of other
ones, part-heard, and everywhere I went, there was a patient,
courteous, private-voiced man sitting on the bench and the
same relaxed, polite, unbureaucratic atmosphere, the same
deliberate effort not to make anyone feel unnecessarily
uncomfortable, frightened or degraded. The fear of Germany
is in my bones. Not only Nazi-Germany. All my life I have
lived with nightmare visions of barrack-loud, dust-bound
German officialdom, immovable, unsmiling, a total negation.
Germany (I spent my earliest childhood there) meant that.
This is another country. It is like having walked into a dream.
What has happened ? Have they changed so much then out of
the ashes ? or reverted to a softer earlier mould ? Was my
image of the Kaiser's Germany a distortion ? or does the
judiciary belong to a different kind ?

A crack of door opens.

" *Ach, der Herr Angeklagte.* Come in, come in ! we've been
waiting for you."

Karlsruhe: The Case of Dr. Brach

" Am I late ? "

" Not at all. *We* are early."

---

6 p.m. Dusk outside. The court choked with people, restive under the harsh electric light. The press are not at their table but posted by the door, messenger boys stand by. Dr. Brach walks in and out, mackintosh over his arm, talking to his lawyer, a free man still. Here too there is now that tension of the coming of the end, that tight feeling of the last minutes of the long wait for the swift last stroke.

When they came in the bench and everybody else remained standing. The judge was covered. He spoke at once.

" In the name of the people—Ulrich Brach has been found Guilty. The sentence of the court is four months prison, this sentence will be deferred for a period of three years." Instantaneously there rose a very ugly growl from the back of the court. The president's voice, trenchant and very loud, cut at once into the swelling sound, " The public will keep quiet. The public plays no part." It ceased as if wiped off. " —If within these three years no new offence has been committed, the prison term will not have to be served. The police must be notified of any change of address. There are no other conditions of probation. The weapon will be confiscated. The defendant will pay the cost of the prosecution." The judge sat down.

Dr. Brach remained where he was. And now began what was in substance a kind of postscriptive summing-up, the *Urteilsbegründung*.

But before the chronological review of the events and the reading of the relevant sections of the Penal Code, the judge brought into the open a smouldering point. He must make it clear at once, he said, that there was no political aspect whatsoever connected with this crime. " The fact that the convicted man happens to be a medical officer of the

Bundeswehr is irrelevant. It has not been of the slightest matter in our finding of the sentence." (Not another peep, this time, out of the back of the court.) The concluding argument ran on these lines : The third shot had neither been justified in law nor necessary in fact. The question of self-defence did not arise as the deceased had never offered the least physical resistance. Even if, as was possible, Dr. Brach had acted under the genuine, though mistaken, belief that the law authorised him to shoot in an emergency, it would still not have been permissible for him to shoot here because *there had been no emergency*, and certainly no compulsory situation, no *Notstandslage*, within the meaning of Paragraph 54. The presence of young Schmitt on the scene ruled out any such interpretation. While there was no doubt that the doctor had acted in a state of considerable excitement, this did not mean that there had been any diminution of his consciousness ; the kind of blacking-out he had suffered immediately after the deed had been limited to a few seconds only.

In mitigation, there had been the doctor's blameless past, and the grim situation which had confronted him as a parent and which had been aggravated by his special medical knowledge of its implications and by his own enforced absences from home. There had also been the fact that due to lack of sleep and a gruelling drive the night before the doctor had been below par on the material day. Furthermore they had had regard to the doctor's present position as the head of a family—there was now a new seven-months old baby—and to the liabilities that might arise out of the legal claim against him by the victim's widow. " In view of all these circumstances, we held a sentence of four months deferred to be the just and sufficient penalty for this deed."

The judge then asked Dr. Brach if he would accept the judgment. Dr. Brach looked at his lawyer.

The lawyer went to him. They would, he said, inform the court of their decision within the legal delay.

" Very good. *Herr Staatsanwalt*—— ? "

Karlsruhe: The Case of Dr. Brach

" We accept."

" Thank you," said the judge, " The hearing is now closed."

When the court was gone, the people cleared out noisily ; the press had left some time ago.

Down the corridor I knocked at one of those doors. This afternoon's public prosecutor was still there.

" The decision," he said, " to appeal or not. Appeal is as of right."

Ad lib ? For either side ?

" For either side."

And they do appeal ? It would seem that one or the other would.

" If they think they can do better in the higher court."

So every case gets heard twice ?

" Most cases are reviewed or re-tried."

Not a new trial ?

" If it is applied for."

So an end is not an end. How very unsettling.

" A trial is one stage of the whole process."

How expensive. And *when* do they make up their mind to accept a judgment ?

" A convicted man may choose to accept at once, or he can take eight days to think it over, *Bedenkzeit*."

What would have happened if Dr. Brach had been sentenced to prison *without* deferment ?

" The same."

Where would he have spent his thinking time ? Also out of jail ?

" Certainly."

A prison sentence then is not immediate ?

" No sentence is legally valid, *rechtskräftig*, before acceptance or appeal."

Even if appeal should take six months ?

" Oh, yes."

And when it does become valid, as supposedly it must one day, what then?

" The convicted man will be notified."

By post?

" In some cases."

You mean nobody is ever whisked away on the spot, whisked away below stairs?

" Please ? "

II

Karlsruhe:
A Plea of Not Guilty

The antecedents of the present German legal system are as chequered as might be expected from the country's general history. The retributory law of the Germanic tribes gradually gave way to Feudal Law and Canon Law, and some centuries later on to Roman Law. By 1532 an elaborate criminal code, the *Constitutio Criminalis Carolina*, was adopted in German territories and remained in force in some parts of them until well into the nineteenth century. The great age of codification, the age of reform and regression after reform, came during the ninety years that followed the French Revolution. Let me fling in some dates to give an idea of the changes and diversities in criminal legislation alone.

Austria adopted a new—and savage—code in 1797, which was somewhat attenuated in 1803 ; Bavaria a more enlightened one in 1813. There was a lull of twenty-five years, then new codes were drafted thick and fast. This was, one must remember, the century of the struggle between German Liberalism and German Absolutism, the conflict between a rising, gifted and enlightened middle-class and the State representing police rule, expanding bureaucracy and a phalanx of pre-constitutional monarchies ; the struggle which ended in German Nationalism, limited monarchy, unlimited bureaucracy, militarism, the supremacy of Prussia and a risen, efficient, money-minded middle-class.

Saxony introduced a new criminal code in 1838, Würtemberg and Sachsen-Weimar-Eisenach in 1839, Hanover and Braunschweig in 1840. Baden and Schwarzburg-Sonder-hausen in 1845 ; and Prussia in 1851. In the Rhineland, the Napoleonic *Code d'Instruction Criminelle* was introduced during the French period and remained in force until 1871.

In the revolutionary summer of 1849 the Kingdom of Würtemberg and the Grand-Duchy of Baden abolished the death penalty by amendment, one hundred years exactly before the present re-abolition by the Federal Republic, and they also abolished all forms of corporal punishment. All were re-introduced by further amendments by 1855.

Prussia was the police state of that time par excellence, with censorship, total ban on foreign newspapers, ban on assembly, political trials, the whole old bag of tricks. Here the martinets managed to hang on to the old code, the *Allgemeine Landrecht* of 1794, until 1851 when it was remodelled in the teeth of violent opposition into the *Neue Strafgestzbuch für die Preussischen Staaten.*

Barely twenty years later, Germany was united under the Kaiser. And so in 1870 the first general German criminal code, the *Reichsstrafgesetzbuch* was drafted and put before the new Reichstag in Berlin. It was informed by many liberal ideas and proposed the abolition of capital punishment throughout the Reich, and it was carried by a vote of 118 to 81. But Bismarck was determined to retain capital punishment and there was a major row. He got his way. It was written into the draft, and the code was passed two months later by 127 votes against 119.

A general German civil Code, the B.G.B., the *Bürgerliche Gesetzbuch*, was established some ten years later, and it is still these two tomes of the Bismarck era which are the law of (West) Germany today. The Twentieth Century brought its changes and additions ; The Weimar Republic inaugurated treatment of juvenile offenders, liberalised divorce, encouraged judicial use of the findings of psychiatry and envisaged very wide reforms indeed in sentencing and procedure, but lacked

Karlsruhe: A Plea of Not Guilty

the stability, the support, the time, to carry them beyond the paper stage ; the Nazis introduced such legislation as served their especial aims—racial decrees, relaxation of the bastardy laws, draconian measures against abortion and homosexuality—, and by their conduct, philosophy and general example diluted and destroyed the rule of justice even where they did not touch its letter ; the Adenauer Republic revived the spirit and restored—with a number of steps forwad— the *status quo ante* of the letter.

———————————

I spent a good part of my remaining time at Karlsruhe in the lower courts as I wanted to see the wheels of daily justice going round. I wanted to watch a turn-over of small cases dealt with single-handed by a judge, but I found that anything like a full equivalent of a day in a London magistrates' court was impossible to come by. Everything took so much longer. The actual pace in court was utterly unflurried ; the case of a purloined bicycle is treated, if perhaps not with quite the thoroughness and repetition of a trial at Assizes, with at least the amount of patience, care and time that would be given to a plea of Not Guilty to a housebreaking charge at Quarter Sessions. And as cases moreover are taken at fixed hours, as we have seen, by appointment as it were, and the timetables are often generous, there are constant intervals of five minutes, ten minutes, the odd half-hour. It appears to be considered less wasteful of time to have the judge and staff wait or have breaks, than oblige parties, solicitors and witnesses to hang about for a portion of their working day. And so while there are about half a dozen summary courts sitting at Karlsruhe from Monday to Friday, the number of cases they get through between them hardly amounts to the number dispatched in the same time by a single London magistrate. How is this practicable ? Of course Karlsruhe is only a place about twice the size of Oxford and half the size of Sheffield, and does not have to cope with anything like a metropolitan list ; however, I found the same deliberateness and spacing later on in the Munich courts, and Munich with a population of about a million is comparable to Manchester or Birmingham. The answer must be that there are more courts and judges to go round in relation to the total work. There are over eleven thousand judges in West Germany (population fifty-two million) as against about a hundred and fifty in England, including County-Court judges and stipendiary magistrates ; but one must not forget that a vast deal of the summary work is done by several thousand lay justices in England.

So far so good. There is another aspect. It is the gap between crime and resolution, the length of time spent awaiting trial. One often hears about this as one of the worst features of Continental justice, but the full, and routine extent of these delays only comes home to one as in case after case one hears the date of the offence. December 1958, it being then October 1959 ; January '59, April '59, September '58. Eight months to a year are standard. In capital offences, particularly if the accused does not admit guilt, it may take two years, three years, before his case is tried. In one instance a man spent four and a half years in prison before his trial (at which he was sentenced to ten years' hard labour). This unrestricted waiting —a very bad thing every way you look at it—does not seem to be caused to any extent by the moderate pace of the trial courts, it is inherent rather in the mechanism and spirit of the criminal prosecution in even a vestigial inquisitorial system, as that system with its predilection for packaged guilt must rely on a lengthy, cautious preliminary investigation conducted by a semi-administrative judiciary, without any positive regard for the passage of time.

That investigation—how does it work, how is it handled ? what are the safeguards ? How does the accused fare during all those months ? The process here, as elsewhere, is not public. One must go by the rules as they stand on paper and by the final look of things in open court.

Karlsruhe: A Plea of Not Guilty

German prosecutions, like ours, are generally set off by the police or (and I believe rather more often than ours) by private denunciation, but it is the local *Staatsanwaltschaft*, the office of public prosecutions, which carries out or orders the initial stages of an investigation. This first inquiry is called an *Ermittelungsverfahren* and it is an indispensable step in every criminal prosecution. The *Staatsanwaltschaft* has no executive organs of its own, but it uses and may give orders to the police. Both may question and generally summon witnesses and suspected persons ; no-one is obliged to answer them.

Inquiries by the *Staatsanwaltschaft* are said to vary in competence according to the size of the police force and the technical facilities at its disposal. As this office is supposed to deal, unfiltered, with everything that happens to crop up, it is bound to waste some time over petty or vindictive rubbish. Not only are the police held to pass on every complaint—in practice they are said to drop a good many— there is also to be found outside the prosecutor's office a large letter slot, like the night-deposit slot of a bank, marked STAATSANWALTSCHAFT in capitals which must be an unwise invitation to persons with a grievance or in liquor.

If an inquiry leads to an arrest, the warrant must be issued by a judge. All arrested persons must be told on arrest the nature of the offence of which they are suspected, and they must be taken to a judge no later than the following day. The judge decides whether or not they are to remain in custody. Bail in our form does not exist ; there is a feeling that money ought not to come into it at all. As a rule custody is ordered whenever there is reason to expect collusion or escape and when there is at the same time a strong *prima facie* case against the man in question. The gravity of the offence is not in itself decisive. A judge is not bound to order custody for a man charged, say, with armed robbery or murder, although in practice he will nearly always do so, unless he should find the *prima facie* case exceptionally weak.

Germany

Now in England it is at this point, when the accused has been arrested and been charged, that his examination comes to an end; he is out of prosecution reach in a faraway prison or at home awaiting trial at the next Sessions or Assizes. It is not so here. The *Staatsanwaltschaft* may now request an *Amtsgerichts* judge—who must comply—to conduct a supplementary inquiry. (The *Staatsanwaltschaft* may neither give nor take orders from the courts, to which it stands in a co-ordinate position, except in this one respect.) This inquiry by a judge is called a *Voruntersuchung*, and is prescribed whenever the case, if committed, would have to go for jury trial; in minor cases, the suspected person as well as the prosecution may apply for it. It appears to have a high reputation for efficiency and lack of bias. (It was abolished by the Nazis in 1935, and re-introduced in 1945.)

A suspected or accused person is entitled not to speak and to refuse to give evidence at all stages of the process, including the ultimate trial, and he must be advised of this right. He may of course be asked the same questions over and over again by the various set-ups.

The judge conducting the inquiry is entirely on his own. Neither the *Staatsanwalt* nor members of his office may be present during an interrogation, while the suspected person, the *Beschuldigte*, may be accompanied by a lawyer. One official witness must be present throughout, and he must be an *Urkundenbeamte*, a record officer under oath. He will be responsible for taking down and summarising the interview. The record must include (see our Judges' Rules) the date, the time, the duration, as well as details of the prescribed formalities observed, and it must be signed by the record officer, the judge and the examined person. If the last refuses, the record must mention this fact and the reason for it. Witnesses are examined singly and alone, and neither the suspected person nor his lawyer may be present. The suspected person may apply for witnesses of his own to be heard, but the judge is not compelled to do so. In fact, at all stages including the trial, witnesses are called or not according to the decision of the court.

When the examining judge decides that he has got to the bottom of it all, he does not come to a conclusion himself, but ties up the dossier and returns it to the *Staatsanwalt* who must now make up his mind. He may stop the whole thing then and there (though having asked for a judicial inquiry, he must get this decision confirmed by a High-court judge) ; in practice a large number of cases are stopped at that stage. If, on the other hand, the *Staatsanwalt* considers that there is a *prima facie* case, he will send an indictment and the dossier to the competent court. This is called *Klage erheben* and is in fact an application for committal. It is now up to the trial judge himself to decide whether the case is to go for trial.

And now the case enters a phase that is sometimes called the *Zwischenverfahren*, the interim process ; the suspected person has now become the accused, the *Angeschuldigte*, and he will be furnished in due course with a copy of the indictment and invited to reply. There will be a prolonged exchange of written matter and possibly another interrogatory session with a judge. Eventually the day will come on which the bench commits [*Eröffnungsbeschluss*]. Dismissal at this stage is very rare. One might say that every case that goes for trial has been pre-tried by judge. On committal, the *Angeschuldigte* becomes automatically the *Angeklagte*—I can offer no nuance of translation—and the tram-lines of justice are now clear.

In the trial courts two things stand out. One, not unexpectedly, is the overwhelming preponderance of cases in which guilt is a foregone and confessed conclusion, the other the enlightened mildness guilt is dealt with. This sheds a double light on the preliminary proceedings down the corridor. I don't mean to suggest that people who admitted guilt were in fact innocent. Any English jury would have convicted every single one of them in ten minutes out on the case presented. The point is that in England the prosecution could seldom have presented so complete a case ; under our rules those people would have had a rather better chance of getting away with it (just as, conversely, some innocent persons would have been filtered out in Germany at an earlier stage and spared a trial). The question is whether this more ample evidence has or has not been " unfairly or oppressively obtained " ?

Oppressive methods do not seem to go with the present climate of the West German legal administration. The examining judges belong to the same service, work in the same building with their colleagues on the trial bench ; they sit some of the time on the trial bench themselves. Mild in word and deeds in public, bullying and barking behind shut doors ? It is base hypothesis, and I doubt it. Unfairness is another matter. An administrative organisation has a huge advantage over any individual. The strain of unlimited probing, however well-conducted, the suspense of months, *are* unfair and a guilty man may well come to prefer to condemn himself out of his own mouth and call it at last a day. The sporting spirit, the notion of the law as a game of skill with handicaps to give each side a chance, is entirely absent on the Continent.

I have had to say confessing or admitting guilt, because I wanted to avoid saying plea of Guilty as there is no such thing. Admission, *Vollgeständigkeit*, is merely a legal mitigation that must be considered in sentencing, but there is no formal distinction between the case of a man who says he is guilty and the case of a man who says that he is not, either are conducted according to the same procedure ; and so it may happen that what in England would be a plea of guilty will be tried in Germany by a judge and jury.

I will try to run through another Karslruhe trial, something typical and brief, a case of, unadmitted, theft in one of the lower courts.

The solo judge in a black gown is alone on the dais except

Karlsruhe: A Plea of Not Guilty

for a girl shorthand-writer who sits next to him. The public prosecutor is in his pulpit ; the accused, also alone, on the front bench. He is a stocky fellow with thick hands. A family of witnesses chattering like starlings are in the witness-room across the passage.

The trial opens with the reading of a circumstantial form of charge. The defendant, whose name is Anton Schweig, is accused of stealing a sum of forty marks, or three pounds ten, in banknotes from a kitchen cupboard in a friend's lodgings.

The judge then begins his examination of the accused, which is divided into two parts. The first is called *zur Person*, concerning the person, and deals extensively with the accused's general circumstances, past and character. This is of course unheard of at an Anglo-Saxon trial where such facts—barring mishaps—are most carefully kept from the knowledge of those who will have to decide between innocence and guilt— magistrates, the jury—and are only disclosed at the end and *after* a conviction, unless indeed his past happens to be very much to the credit of the accused in which case it might be brought up by the defence and thereby become liable to cross-examination. But whenever the facts run like these, "He's a single man, your Lordship, twenty six years of age, of no fixed employment, there are four previous convictions——", they are heard only from the police officer in the box who steps up like Fortinbras after the cards are down. Here it is done first off and by the judge himself.

"You're twenty-six ? Oh, twenty-seven this month . . . Born in '32 you were then ? Hmhm. School ? Seven years elementary, hmhm. Learn any trade ? No . . . What did you do on leaving school ? "

" I worked for the Americans."

" You worked for the Americans . . . Parents alive ? "

" Mother."

" Yes, I see—your father was killed in Russia. You have two brothers, one sister, all married—you don't live at home—

work—what about work ? You're employed as a lorry driver
now ? What have you been earning ? "

"Well," says Schweig, " it depends . . ."

The judge flips a page. " Changing jobs pretty frequently . . .
Laying off work . . . How is that ? "

Shrug.

" What do you do when you don't work ? "

" Don't know. Go about on my motor-bike."

" Have you had any previous convictions ? "

The young man puts his hands behind his back. Silence.
". . . well, yes."

" How many ? "

" Must I tell ? "

" I'm afraid so. That's a rule."

There is no jury to hear it. Only, besides the judge and the
shorthand girl, the prosecutor and a sprinkling of audience
in the back of the court. There are no reporters ; press
attendance, unless the case has news value, is always meagre.
The accused is not represented.

" One or two. But no prison. I've never been to prison."

" It is quite true that you were never *in* prison," says the
judge, " you had two deferred prison sentences, and before
these one fine and one sentence of week-end youth arrest—
you had four previous convictions, all for stealing. Is that so?"

" I didn't do it, not the last time."

" I see that you appealed. The *Oberlandesgericht* confirmed
the original conviction."

The accused slumps down on the bench, a stubborn look
on his face.

" *Zur Sache*," says the judge, concerning the issue. This
marks the opening of the second part of the examination.
" Herr Schweig—you heard what you are accused of, what
have you to say about it ? "

Herr Schweig stands up again. "I didn't touch Frau
Ludwig's forty marks. Honest I didn't."

" Will you tell us exactly what happened. Take your time."

Karlsruhe: A Plea of Not Guilty

It was a Wednesday, in October, just a year ago, he wasn't working, he thought he might as well run out to Hemsbach and pay a visit to the Ludwigs.

" You knew them well ? "

Oh, yes. Ludwig had been his mate at one time, he'd been to their wedding . . .

" Did you often go to see them ? "

Every now and then.

" So on that day you drove to the village of Hemsbach. At what time did you get there ? "

About noon. Ludwig wasn't home, he was out working. Frau Ludwig said now that he'd come he might as well stay, she would fix him something to eat. And so she did. And so he stayed.

" Where was that ? "

In the kitchen. Well, they ate, and then Frau Ludwig said she was going to make some coffee, she was expecting mother to come in. They talked about this and that and the other and Frau Ludwig said how she'd saved up forty marks out of the housekeeping money because she was saving for a new cooker and how she was keeping it in two twenty-mark notes in a cigarette-box in the kitchen cupboard, and not to tell her husband.

" Did she actually show you the box ? "

The box, and the money inside. She put it back under some napkins and stuff, and said not to tell her husband. And then Frau Scholl, that's the mother, came in and they drank some coffee, and later on Frank Sontag came in with his girl, he was the Ludwigs' under-lodger, and Frau Ludwig said she'd fix them something to eat, and Frank said he'd just run across to get some sausage and Ruth, that's Frank's girl, said she'd come with him and Frau Scholl said she must be going anyhow and Frau Ludwig said, " I'll see you out, Mother," and she said for him to wait as she was going to make more coffee. Well, then he thought it was getting kind of late and, well, he decided to leave, well, he decided to leave and he left.

" At what point exactly did you leave the kitchen, Herr Schweig ? "

It must have been on four o'clock or thereabouts.

" Did you leave *with* the others or after them ? "

Just after them ; Frau Ludwig had told him to stay and drink some more coffee and then he saw how late it was and he left.

" Were you alone in the kitchen for any time ? "

Oh, yes. Just for a minute or so.

" Did you see Frau Ludwig again before you left ? "

Oh, yes. She and her mother were standing downstairs, talking in the doorway. He said good-bye and went home. Drove off on his motor-bike.

" Was anything said to you about your leaving being unexpected ? "

Oh, no. He didn't think there was. Just told them he couldn't wait for Ludwig any longer. He told them that. Oh yes. And went home. It was late and he went home.

" Anything else, Herr Schweig ? "

No. Except I never touched the money.

" Thank you," said the judge. " We will now hear the witnesses." Frau Ludwig, Herr Ludwig, Frau Scholl, Frank Sontag and Ruth walked in with a great air of suppressed excitement. The judge gave them the customary instructions in plain terms and sent them out again. Frau Ludwig remained. She was a strapping housewife of about twenty-five or six, very clean and neat, with a high colour and not a trace of make-up.

Oh, she says, there wasn't much to tell.

Yes, he came that Wednesday. My husband was out to work. Naturally. He said he had nothing else to do and would wait for my husband.

" What time did you expect your husband back ? " asks the judge.

At six o'clock of course. A quarter past six, time for him to get home.

Karlsruhe: A Plea of Not Guilty

" Herr Schweig was a friend ? "

Friend? No . . . Yes . . . We knew him quite well.

" He frequently came to see you in your home ? "

Oh, he did.

" And you trusted him ? "

Pardon ? I don't think we thought about it.

Her story squares with Schweig's to the stage of the mass
exodus.

" When you went downstairs you left the accused in the
kitchen ? "

Yes.

" Alone ? "

Oh, yes. He was going to wait for my husband. I was
coming back to make some more coffee.

" How long was he alone ? "

Perhaps a few minutes. I was standing outside with
mother, we were talking, when I heard Herr Schweig running
down the stairs, I don't think he could see us. ' What's the
matter ? ' I said, ' Oh,' he said, ' I need to go to the toilet.'
' Then you've come to the wrong place,' I said, ' have you
forgotten it's upstairs ? ' We share the toilet with the landlord,
it's on the landing one flight up. So he turned and went
up stairs.

" Did he go up to the lavatory ? "

Well we thought he did. He was back quite soon. He
said how it was late and he must go now. I said, ' Aren't you
going to wait for my husband ? ' but he said no he couldn't
and he was gone.

So then she and mother went on talking for a little while ;
and Ruth and Frank came back, and Ruth had got some eggs,
" Frau Ludwig," she had said, " may I fix them for him ?
Frank hasn't had his dinner yet ", and so they went upstairs.

Presently they left ; presently her husband returned ; and
at ten o'clock that evening she discovered that the money in
the cupboard was no longer there.

When had she seen it last ? asked the judge.

" When I showed it to Herr Schweig, at noon."

" Had you looked for it since then ? "

" No."

" Why did you look for it when you did ? "

" I was going to bed and I just wanted to put my hand on it."

" Any particular reason ? " She shakes her head. " You mean you did this every night ? "

" Yes."

" Frau Ludwig—I want you to think about this very carefully. Between four p.m. when Herr Schweig left, and ten p.m. when you discovered the theft, who was in, or had access to your kitchen ? "

Frank and Ruth for about half an hour, but they were never alone. Ludwig after six o'clock for the whole of the evening, and he was sometimes alone. Nobody else came, nobody else had access. A plan of the premises is produced by the court and discussed. The Ludwigs' lodgings were on the first floor of a three-storey house and consisted of the kitchen and a bedroom. The kitchen was reached by a door—and by that door only—from a passage. The bedroom led out from the kitchen and had no other exit. There were two more rooms on that floor ; one of them was also rented by the Ludwigs who sublet it to young Frank, the other was occupied by the landlord's son. The landlord and his wife lived on the top-floor, and the ground-floor was occupied by a dairy.

" Between four p.m. and ten, Frau Ludwig, were you ever out of your kitchen ? "

I must have been. I don't remember, it's over a year ago . . . But it doesn't matter because nobody could have come into our kitchen when I was out, nobody, because I always lock it. My husband does, too. We each have our key.

"Yes," says the judge, he sees. "But—*always* ? People don't always lock their doors when they step out for a minute or two."

Oh yes, we do. We always do. We are on bad terms with our landlord and I always lock our kitchen. When I hang

out the washing in the yard I do. I keep the key in my apron.
Our kitchen is always locked, even when I go up to the toilet
I lock it.

The judge calls the mother. It is the same story. Frau
Scholl (rotund, comfortable; scrubbed face, hair in bun,
laced boots) left the kitchen with her daughter, stood in the
doorway talking, when down in a great clatter came Herr
Schweig—he must be in a hurry, I said to my daughter, my
daughter laughed and asked him if he had forgotten his way
about the house, so up he went and hardly a minute later
he was down again and out of the house and gone.

" Did he say anything before he left ? "

Adieu und dankeschön.

" Call Herr Ludwig, please," says the judge. Frau Ludwig
beckons to her mother who settles herself next to her on the
witness bench.

Ludwig looks a lively, friendly sort of chap, wiry and
short, with an ugly, mobile face. He is dressed in a short brown
leather jacket. He was going to bed, he said, when he heard
a shriek : the money was gone. (He turns round to look at
his wife for confirmation. She gives him a broad wink.) He
calmed her down, and they decided to sleep over it. Next
morning first thing she went to tell her mother. " My mother-
in-law came over and she said to me, she said, ' Perhaps Herr
Schweig took the money, he's got a lot against him.' ' Jesus-
Sakrament, the silly louse ! ' I said, ' we'd better ask him.'
If he took it, it must have been some sort of prank, you know,
I thought. I had to get to work, so I phoned and left a message,
I knew where to get him, it's a place he takes his meals . . .
I said how something had happened yesterday and we wanted
to speak to him and how it was urgent, and would he contact
my wife. But he didn't show up. I phoned again in the evening
and the woman said she'd seen him. Three times in all I
phoned and on Saturday morning my wife and my mother-
in-law went to the police."

Herr Ludwig joined the witness bench. Then came the

two local police officers who had investigated the complaint. It was they who had drawn the house plan and who now confirmed it. And last came the two young people, Ruth and Frank, who had nothing to add except corroboration and the impression they made, which was that of two people who have nothing to hide and are on easy terms with themselves and all the world.

They had heard the next morning. They didn't think of Herr Schweig; they didn't know what to think. Later: yes. When he didn't turn up. "Well, in his place I would have turned up if I was innocent."

Throughout, the judge listens without comment. "What do you know about the locking of that kitchen door ? " he asks.

"It was always locked," says Frank Sontag, " I couldn't get in when Frau Ludwig was out. Something to do with the Ludwigs having had a row with the landlord's wife."

Was there anything in that which might concern the matter here ?

"Oh no, no. Just one of those things."

"Now, Herr Schweig," says the judge, " do you wish to say anything about the witnesses' evidence ? ask them any questions ? "

Herr Schweig stands up. "I don't know why it must be me ! Why don't you ask *him* ? " He points at Ludwig.

Instant derisive cackling from the witness bench. Frau Ludwig springs forward.

"*My* husband doesn't have to steal the housekeeping money ! he can ask me. It's his money, he earns it——"

"My son-in-law, Herr Richter, let me tell you——"

"Ask him if he isn't a well-known spender," shouts Schweig, " ask him if he's ever managed to save a *pfennig* piece, ask him ! "

"Herr Ludwig," the judge calmly asks, " did you take your wife's money ? "

Ludwig stands up and grins. " ' Course not." Again he turns to catch her eye ; both giggle.

" He did," says Schweig. " His own wife said to me not to tell him about her money."

" That's a lie——"

" My daughter, Herr Richter——"

" ' Course I knew she had the money, I knew she was saving for a cooker, I didn't know where she kept it, I didn't ask."

The judge says, " Are you on good terms with your wife ? "

Hilarity amongst the clan. " We get on all right."

" Is there any truth in the allegation that you spend money rather too freely ? "

" Oh, I don't know . . ."

" Would you say you were *careful* with money ? "

" Careful, no." Another glance behind him.

" Are you hard up ? "

" No."

" Not at the beginning of the week," supplements his wife.

" What do you do with your money ? Do you smoke ? " There is a tax on cigarettes in Germany, nearly as high as ours.

" Not much."

" Do you drink ? "

" No."

" He likes to eat, and he spends a lot on fruit," says the wife.

Schweig says, " Ask him if *he* hasn't got a record ! "

" You realize that it is my duty—in the circumstances of this case—to ask you this. Have you any previous convictions ? "

" No——o."

" Quite positive ? "

" No——o."

" I must warn you that this is a matter that can easily be verified."

" Just motoring. [Relaxing into a smirk] Dangerous driving, two times—that's not dishonourable ? "

Germany

"Oh quite," says the judge, "that doesn't constitute a criminal record. No bearing on this case whatsoever. Thank you." Then suddenly recollecting, he adds, "Not that you should take these convictions lightly—dangerous driving is a very serious matter indeed."

"No criminal record——" mutters Schweig, "what about that other little matter?" He says it so much under his breath that one cannot be certain one has heard it. The women must have: for an instant—another uncertain impression—they looked scared.

The judge now asked the witnesses to step forward, and administered a collective oath. Meanwhile the morning had been getting on and he declared a short adjournment.

The Ludwig contingent kept together in a whispering bunch. "—the cheek—did he mean?—so you think he meant—? [I think I caught, I can almost swear I did, the word abortion] —Anyway you weren't married then, children, so it didn't count. I should have boxed his ears. You should have walked over and boxed his ears." Herr Ludwig turned to me, "Ought I to have boxed his ears? You are from the Welfare Bureau?"

"No," I said and, "no."

The two police officers, who had given evidence, came over in their green and belted uniforms. One of them said, "Are you a hundred per cent sure nobody else could have got in that afternoon?"

The other, a middle-aged man, said, "You must think hard— you do know, don't you, that this time it would be prison for him? *Es geht um die Freiheit.* If you've got any little doubt you must tell. You don't want to have it on your conscience." The Ludwigs looked crestfallen and serious.

Schweig stood alone in the passage, trying to look at nothing, lighting a cigarette.

Then someone came to say that if they wanted witness-money now was the time to go downstairs and sign the claims. "*Zeugengeld?*" they said and looked at the policemen. "For loss of work and your transport." And down they all trooped.

The rest was quick. The public prosecutor spoke soberly for ten minutes, summing up the facts. He submitted that there was no doubt that the accused had committed the offence—he had had ample opportunity, furthermore the manner of his leaving and his subsequent behaviour were plain *indicia* of guilt. In aggravation, there were his previous record, his persistent denials, his attempt to put the guilt upon another and, above all, the element of breach of trust which entered into this offence : the accused had been received into the Ludwigs' home with the hospitality and confidence accorded to a trusted friend. The prosecution's submission therefore must be a conviction and a prison sentence of eight months.

" Herr Schweig, the last word is yours."

But the accused had reached the stage of deflation.

" What *is* your submission ? "

? ? ?

" Your submission is acquittal ? *Sie beantragen Freispruch* ? "

" *Ja.*"

The judge retired alone for ten minutes ; walked in again and standing, read, " *Im Namen des Volkes*—Anton Schweig, born on the seventh third nineteen-hundred and thirty-two at Tuttingen in the County of Wolfach [these delaying bureaucratics are prescribed procedure] is convicted of larceny involving the sum of forty D-Marks, the sentence of the court is five months prison." In arriving at this decision, the judge said, the court had had to consider several factors, and the most decisive of these had been the convicted man's character. Opportunity—? Certainly he had had opportunity, but it had not been an exclusive opportunity, other persons also had had access to the money in the box. Herr Ludwig had had access ; a number of persons unknown might have had access. Frau Ludwig had been very certain that she always locked her door and she had told the court that she had what might be called a strong human motive for doing so.

The Ludwigs and attendants were now sitting good and quiet, hands folded, their mouths faintly open.

Even so, there could have been a slip, people were often convinced that they *always* did a certain thing when in fact they only did it eight times out of ten. The lock and key in question were an ordinary kind of lock and key ; there was a shop downstairs and the house appeared to have been at all times full of people coming and going. He must say here that this did not mean that suspicion fell on any specific person and particularly not upon Herr Ludwig. Herr Ludwig, in the court's opinion, could safely be ruled out. Unless he and all the witnesses were veritable monsters of deceit, and very accomplished actors as well—and there was not a scrap of evidence that they were either—it was in the highest degree unlikely that Herr Ludwig should have laid hands on his wife's savings in the kitchen cupboard. So when he said that the convicted man had not had exclusive opportunity, he meant neither more nor less than that Schweig was not the only person who had had access, and that so there remained an element of doubt.

A doubt, the judge went on, which according to the normal experience of life would have been strengthened if anything by the manner—an extremely childish and incompetent manner—in which the theft would have been carried out if it had in fact been perpetrated by Schweig. Frau Ludwig had shown him the bank notes ; he had been alone in the kitchen ; he had practically run away in the middle of a visit ; he had failed to communicate again—every single step would point to him. And when one added to this that he was a man with a number of previous convictions of theft against him, did it not become at least doubtful that such a man—a man, mind you, not a boy, a man of twenty-six—should choose to commit such a theft with such a record and in such circumstances and hope to get away with it ? Was it not, if he might express it so, almost a little too pat? This doubt, however, had been conclusively dispelled by the character of this man's previous convictions.

Here, the judge said, he must give a warning, it would be very wrong indeed to assume that because a man had some past convictions this was always and necessarily an indication of present guilt. " *He's got a lot against him.*" Convictions might be one kind of indication, and they might also indicate the opposite. Some men were capable of committing one kind of offence and incapable of committing another. Once a criminal, always a criminal was emphatically not so in the view of this court. Sometimes it might be just such a previous warning that caused a man to turn over a new leaf.

In the present case, however, the court had found that every one of the convicted man's former thefts had been of precisely the same nature : stupid, impulsive actions prompted by some sudden temptation, doomed to failure. And they had failed. And it was so that the court had come to the inevitable conclusion that in the highest degree of probability the theft had been committed by the man accused. The court also agreed with the prosecution view that by far the most aggravating element of the offence was the abuse of trust. It was in many ways a distressing case. One might say that the convicted man lacked to a marked degree in control and common powers of reflection, in other words that he was foolish and weak, but folly and weakness did not in law diminish his responsibility for his actions. " Herr Schweig, will you accept the judgment ? Or do you wish to appeal ? "

Schweig says he wants to think it over.

" Very good. You have eight days."

Schweig picks up his cap. " Good-bye," he says, and sidles out of court.

The Ludwig clan move off as if they were leaving church.

III

Notes

Scene : The Federal Court of Justice in full session, the highest court in the land, housed beyond marbled halls like the head office of a major bank—a lofty room, chandeliers, a crescent of Supreme-Court Judges, robed in purple, portrait-faced; the drone of trained voices. No extraneous presence mars the legal surface. Appellants do not appear. The Presiding Judge, the Chief Justice of the day is a woman. A tiny sound; something has slid on the carpet; the Chief Justice has dropped a pencil, the Chief Justice bends and picks it up.

Women. The Weimar Republic abolished a number of their disabilities; the Nazis sent them back again into the kitchen. The most conscientious of new brooms, the Federal Republic, has promulgated absolute feminine equality in a recent decision of the Constitutional Court at Karlsruhe. Among all other things, this means equal civil-service pay; it means that the father can no longer overrule the mother on a question concerning a child's education (which rather places the child between two bundles of hay); and it means that women may now stand for any—except ecclesiastical—office.

" Members of the jury, you are men and women of the world ! Common sense will tell you . . ." One does not often hear a speech made in an English court that does not have recourse to these two stand-bys. In Germany, the men of the world and their common sense are replaced by experience of life, *Lebenserfahrung* and *Erfahrungstatsachen* are great favourites of bench and bar. Their status is quasi-judicial. In a case I heard reviewed, the appellant had been given a stiff prison sentence for running over two very drunk pedestrians and killing one of them. It had been night, the motorist was going along at twenty-five or thirty miles an hour, some distance ahead two men were wobbling arm-in-arm across the road. They reached the further pavement. But no sooner safe than they stepped back again into the road and smack into his car. In the judgment it was held that the motorist was responsible, not because he had not driven with ordinary due care, but because he had failed, if you please, to exercise the extraordinary care incumbent upon him in the circumstances. The day had been Carnival-Monday, *Rosenmontag ;* common experience of life must have taught him that if one saw two middle-aged gentlemen arm-in-arm upon the road on Carnival-Monday night, it became one's legal duty to proceed with extraordinary care. (An opinion not upheld on appeal.)

Konstanz. A case of armed robbery with assault had taken place in the tap-room of an inn. How had it started, when did the accused come in ? The accused had been there all evening, sitting drinking with the other guests. At midnight the accused, with ten years in sentences for heavy crimes behind him and who might have learnt some discretion, turned off the light switches and began to sing : *Lichter aus—Messer raus !* Lights out—knives out.

Lindau/Bodensee. A customs case. Someone, eighteen months ago, brought 235 cigarettes into the country instead of the allowed 200. The judge and prosecutor who have to cope with this, and who dealt sensibly enough with other matters earlier in the morning, turn into unworldly sticklers. Prompted by the customs representative, they pore over the letter of the regulations but choose to ignore the facts of modern travel.

Almost any kind of case, however trivial, that comes before the courts involves some rudiment of a valid issue, capable (ideally) of a satisfactory and just solution. Not so customs and excise cases. There is something pettifogging and rapacious as well as extremely irritating about these actions anywhere. They are unbecoming to a country, as traffic in wax candles is unbecoming to a great church. It is no help to say that these niggling rules and their techniques of application are the law of the land; they were slipped most likely into some finance bill before anyone could have said Member for Kidderminster. Try to find the M.P., or Deputy or Member of Congress or the *Bundesrat*, who will, or can, do anything about it. " If it please your Lordship—this concerns an attempt to defraud Her Majesty by concealment of four fifths of a pint of fortified fermented beverage known by the trade-name of Dubonnet." Indeed. It sounds more like Shylock *v.* Indifferent Honest Citizen.

Court day at Staufen (market town, 3000 inhabitants) at the edge of the Black Forest. A young judge—first appointment —who is not always certain of the local dialect, sits behind a desk in a small, neat office smelling of fresh paint, hearing a calendar of civil claims. Outside a pig squeals long and loud. These were the litigants, in order of appearance.

1) Two scraggy sisters in alpaca overalls *v.* a slovenly man and wife, refugees from some Prussian hinterland in the East Zone—landladies and (compulsory) tenants engaged in a running row re-enacted here at the top of voices. Coal in the hall—*and* his bicycle—the woman—never switches it off— the filth—at all hours—you cannot please those old bitches— the slut—let me tell you—washing her hair in the middle of the night—— Round goes the canon, and in the lulls the young judge tries to insert a mollifying suggestion and is shouted down. Die Frau—der Mann—der Dreck—die ist so—der ist so—

die alten Hexen—die Drecksau—erstunken und erlogen—
immer—nimmer—nie—nein——

After twenty minutes the judge manages to get down a
form of resolution : the tenants will try their best to find
lodgings of their own (Oh, haven't they !), the court will
second their application with the Housing Bureau ; meanwhile
landladies and tenants will try to live on better terms. This
starts another round.

" Live and let live," says the judge. (" Not with those
witches ! ") Perhaps, he says, the Fräulein should try not to
scold *all* the time. They pinch their lips.

They shuffled out. " Folk music," the judge said to his
scribe ; a waiting lawyer called after the sour sisters, " You
two ought to drink more wine."

2) Two lawyers, one for a dentist, the other for his
patient. The new false teeth don't work ; they won't bite.
They were not meant to bite, pleads the dentist's man, they
were ordered for best, a Sunday-afternoon set. The judge
adjourns the case.

3) An almost incomprehensible man, telling a story in
deepest gutturals about the man from his village whom he
saw and did not see again on the Russian Front. (The least
healed of all recent German memories.) That man had been
missing these fourteen years ; his wife and son are trying to
establish his death. The witness is gnarled and used by work,
and it comes as a shock to learn that he was born in 1916.
Villichichilickey, he says, that's where he saw the dead soldier,
only he was not dead then ; himself he was only passing
through on leave, on his way home, he was off to marry,
d'Hochziet mache. Oh, yes, that was where he saw him,
it was *him* marching by. . . . Judge and scribe tumble to
Velikiye Luki ; but not much else can be established.

4) Two peasant women, mother and daughter, against a
company lawyer with a well-filled briefcase. Breach of contract.
They haven't paid for their washing machine. The lawyer
produces the signed documents ; the women tell the story.

Germany

This is how it was, Herr Doktor, the gentleman came with the machine, not this gentleman, another gentleman from the company. He said he would demonstrate a wash. They fetched some sheets. The machine was doing its stuff, the gentleman talked, got out the forms. Mother went off to milk, the daughter stayed and watched. When mother came back from the cows, the sheets had been torn into shreds.

"And grey, Herr Doktor, not a clean wash."

But the contract by then was signed. (They always do, said the judge.) This case, too, was adjourned.

5) Another housing case. There is, as one quickly comes to realize, still a painful shortage in Germany. They build as hard and fast as they can, which is fast, but haven't been able to catch up yet, and this is not made easier by the steady weekly arrivals of refugees from the East Zone. Thus here, a couple quartered on another in a three-room flat. Four grown-ups and five children share this and one kitchen. They have not come to quarrel, they have come to ask the court to assist them with the Bureau.

"Oh, you are agreed?" says the judge. "Good." He arranges for the landlord to make out an eviction order. This will not enable him to evict the tenants, but it might enable *them* to get another place to live. The parties do not entirely like the sound of this stratagem, but bow to departmental logic.

6) Far-fetched witnesses travelled from other towns to give evidence in a small-scale Captain von Köpenik affair. During the war a civil servant had been sent to Poland to administer some department as an under-secretary. The Russians came, the war was lost, so were the files, the official went home, having meanwhile been promoted to deputy-secretary. He had lived respectably ever after, doing the work, drawing the salary, scoring the pension proper to his rank, until some recent bureaucratic treasure trove cast a dubious light. A self-awarded promotion? Suspended, he has now advertised up and down the Occupied and Unoccupied Zones

Notes

for witnesses of his Polish triumph : the colleague, last heard of at Breslau, who had seen the telegram ; the couple, then next door, who had shared the opened bottle. . . .
" There are dozens of these cases," said the judge.

Moses [Heirs] v. *Deutsches Reich*. In every German town of any size there sit, almost continuously, the *Rückerstattungs-kammern*, the Courts of Restitution. Most of the plaintiffs are dead. Their traceable descendants are settled in the United States, in Israel, in England. The claims are for possessions torn from them between the years of 1933 and 1944. A Turkey carpet driven off by the S.S.; a brooch and two gold rings confiscated in a precious-metals drive ; a Bechstein Grand ; a wireless set . . . A boy's motor bicycle . . . A fur coat taken away by the Gestapo after a morning raid. . . . Anyone who cares to, may walk in and hear, this is the aftermath of what everybody knew, and here it is going on, in living memories. And it is as grim and pitiful and unbearable as it ever was.

The plaintiffs in such cases are represented more often than not by Jewish law firms. Once more, Jewish faces are seen in German courts ; Jewish lawyers move, speak, mix, with apparent smoothness. " Morning, Herr Colleague——" " Morning, dear sir——" All as before ? Better than before ? Whatever lies behind—must lie behind—this is a daily reality.

Is the past then healing ? Forgiving and self-forgiving are graces, mysterious and individual, hard-won or sudden, always incalculable. There are some explicit signs of acceptance and realisation, of what the Germans themselves would call insight ; there is also much bleating and shifting of blame— we were misled, we did not know, we had no idea. Perhaps the past is simply falling behind through the passage and surge of life, through distraction, the monkey-shift of mind, the plain human inability to keep it up, the inevitable final slackening of everything. There is also something more positive. The past is put behind because men and women have *in fact* turned over a new leaf; there *is* the change. Recoil from calamity and horror, recoil, also and naturally, from insupportable guilt, is taking the form of deeds. There *is* the new regard for life—it would be hard for a Bismarck to-day to reintroduce the death penalty—there is the respect of man for man, the tending of liberty and the decencies and the due process of law, and with it goes a love, an almost avid love, of normality and all its trimmings.

A change—yes. But is it not a most opportunistic one, a new conformity? Certainly; as far as that goes. Does not social conduct follow at all times, not perhaps the leader, but the prevailing wind of change? Social conduct is contagious; there is mass contagion by a good rule just as there is mass contagion by a bad one, although there are always contributory factors, nobody needs to catch it; a great many always do catch it. It is an unwise man who is sure of his own immunity.

In Germany there is now another factor. Time. Not time the healer, but sheer time, quantitative time. When people like myself think of Germany to-day, they think of post-Nazi Germany, a country of ex-Nazis, surviving anti-Nazis and victims. In fact, this can only apply to a limited and diminishing number of people. I have just made some calculations. Hitler took over in 1933; the régime ended in 1945, twelve years later. Anyone in Germany to-day under the age of thirty has nothing to forget (except childhood hardships); anyone between thirty and forty-five was from three to eighteen years old when Hitlerism began.

What about the rest, the rest that counts, since notoriously we are all run by men of over fifty-five, to put it young. Are there any Nazis left in Germany? Obviously, yes. They cannot all be dead; they cannot *all* have changed. What about the allegations that important Nazis are still or once more in high government positions? I do not know. I have no facts or impressions to speculate on. What about the alleged two hundred Nazi judges still sitting on the bench? Again, I do not know. That among some eleven thousand German judges two hundred—at least !—must have been active Nazis, like it or not, makes common sense. Question, are these two hundred supposed to be Nazis now or Nazis then? Men with a past who have discarded it, or men who think and feel and wish as Nazis still? In that case they must be Nazis in good judges' clothing.

IV

Munich: Summary Justice— A German Divorce

In Munich the Palace of Justice—such is the name—is a florid, pompous pile of 1870 baroque and forms the centre-piece of a loud square. Even so courts, archives and offices spill over into an annexe laid out like an ornate railway station. The clientele is large and mixed. Munich, before the war, before it had become the present phantasmagoric and quite ominous exhibit of destruction, the jumble of boomtown with black, solid ruins and the standing *pezzi grossi* of Wittelsbach Victorian masonry, must have been a curious place, very German and unlike any other place in Germany. It was, and is, the sophisticated, hybrid capital of a mountainous and rural country on the wrong side of the Alps. For in aspiration Munich is incurably Italianate, an expression in flesh and stone of that perennial Germanic longing, *der Drang nach dem Süden*. Only whereas the architects and the good citizens and the building prince dreamed of Florence, what the people tried to live was Naples. Pace and life were set by an extravagant, operatically romantic and beloved court (and later on by the memories of that court), by a middling and on the whole not very prosperous, intensely local aristocracy (*Graf* and groom to this day wear the same Bavarian dress), a large number of academic figures who had come by choice, a very large number of artists, and by a robust, pious, rowdy, beer-swilling populace of artisans and shop-

154

keepers, Catholics to the bone, swaying through the year in a round of saturnalia—an eight weeks' open carnival, roast oxen at the fair—punctuated by prescribed lean days.

The very beer is brewed strong or thin according to the Apostolic Calendar. It was a Munich rabble that first attached itself to Hitler. The King was often mad ; the Regent behaved with marked eccentricity. All the professors were respectable and most of them were eminent. Thomas Mann settled here, his own compromise possibly between his brand of Mediterranean longings and his need for a discipline of the North. Many of the artists were thriving and respected artist figures ; the crowd of them were artists by dress and habits : Munich had the second largest pre-war population of painters in the world, Paris with a round hundred thousand coming first. The streets were always full of tourists, tourists en route for Italy, tourists setting out on climbs, English and American tourists come to stay, imbued with the same kind of love for Munich the inhabitants bear the land beyond the Brenner Pass. The climate is not good; wet cold alternates with summer rain, dry days are scourged by a southern wind called Föhn that flays the nerves (in crimes of violence Föhn is always put forward in mitigation) ; the *Loggia dei Lanzi*—what is left of it—looks dusty, heavy, philistine and what it is : a nineteenth-century copy ; pavements and drinking cellars have indeed achieved some *débraillé*, but it is not that of Donatello's Mercury, smiles here are guffaws, the rugged feasting is not even Murrillon, it has a Flemish streak, it is Brueghel. And yet there are blue days and those are of a quality, so rare, so luminous, so alien, that one can see what the inhabitants have hoped to see for so many hundred years.

To-day, Munich looks as gutted as London did in 1945. The Brown House is a shell ; Königliche Hoheit has receded to the point of no return, though Wagner, Lola Montez and King Ludwig keep marching on in nostalgic memory. The rest is there. The fair-ground crowds ; the dishes heaped with gross farinaceous eating—dumplings and sausage, and cabbage and fat; the magnificent art collections; the professors; a bohemia in new clothes; the aristocracy, fewer, older, leaner, more very old women than men, more down-at-heel after every war; the tourists re-inforced now by swarms of Balkan refugees and by the omnipresence, in uniform and out, of the *Amerikaner*, all milling between the cosy pre-fabs with the little theatre and the good shops and the gap-blown, rectilinear streets of bourgeois tenements, and of course the Beer Halls.

The Beer Halls are hideous. The Beer Halls have to be seen to be believed. They are the Corner Houses of a different world. Bavarian beer as we all know is very good indeed. A difference in degree makes a difference in kind. Here it becomes something vile. At the Hofbräu, at the Löwenbräu, the Salvator, the Augustiner, hundreds upon hundreds of men and women sit each with a two-pint pot of beer before them, and down the aisles there open, flight on flight, ample, Roman, marbled, loud with gushing waters, the urinals and the vomitoria.

As for the country, it is here that the foothills of the Alps begin, the region of Europe that has always been inhabited—whether, on paper, Swiss or Austrian or Bavarian—by a stock of strong and narrow peasant strain. It is the goitre belt of prudish Catholicism, guttural speech, unkindness to animals, endurance, craft, frugality, cretins and hard-worked women. There are as always contradictions. There is Baroque art, the white and golden, lyrical architecture of these lands. There is the fact that this one of the loveliest, most elegant, original, and surely recondite, of European styles sprang from and flourished in these deceptively uncouth regions.

The Munich courts, high and low, operate in two distinct sets, one with jurisdiction over Munich Town, the other over Munich Land. The lists of both are heavy (at least while I was there) with sexual offences and crimes of violence: procuration, assault, abortion, in an unhappy conjunction of native tendencies with the ubiquitous *Amerikaner.*

" You must have known that he was married ? " the judge says to the girl.

" He was going to divorce for me."

" And when you had the second baby, the one that lived—luckily for you—the one that was born last month, that was by him, too ? "

She is getting on for nineteen by now. The first one, the one she managed not to have, would have come when she was still in law a juvenile. (The mills of Continental justice.)

" Where is he now ? " says the judge.

" I don't know."

There is information, the prosecution puts in, that he was taken into custody by the U.S. military authority.

The judge is sitting with two jurors, round-eyed, sausage-fingered men who do not utter.

The girl volunteers, " He sold his TV set to pay for the doctor's fee." The doctor, too, is in custody.

The judge says, " What are we to do with you ? Didn't you know that this was serious ? Didn't you know that for adults it can mean hard labour ? Didn't you look it up ? "

The girl shakes her frizzy head.

The public prosecutor, a small dark man with a foreign accent, a political refugee from a Rumanian province, speaks and asks for a sentence of four weeks juvenile detention.

" A load off your mind ? " says the judge. Cat-and-mouse or kindliness ? One cannot quite tell.

They discuss what would be the most convenient time for doing the four weeks. The girl has got a job as chambermaid at an hotel; December is the slack season. The prosecutor says it would be more desirable really if she spent Christmas at home with the new baby. The judge concurs. All this, it must be noted, takes place before sentencing.

What about January then ? January is cleaning time. The spring ? That's the beginning of the season. The father is in

Germany

court, a great big wood-hewn Bavarian with a game leg, sobbing heartily. Please, he says, will they give her a deferred sentence.

The judge explains that the law does not allow him to defer a sentence of juvenile detention. A prison sentence might be deferred, but the minimum prison sentence prescribed for this offence is six months.

What does it matter, says the father, as long as it is deferred.

(A sentence to a term of prison deferred is the Continental form of our conditional or suspended sentence. In a case where we might give, say, a twelve months' conditional discharge or a year's probation, they would make it a month prison deferred for one year. The principle is the same ; the convicted person is given a complete chance and in either form is liable to go to prison if he relapses. The practical effect may well be different : it is likely that the knowledge of a definite sentence, of the month in the book, has a greater deterrent influence than the remembered words, " If there is a new charge you can be brought here again and be punished for this charge ").

The judge says that unfortunately it is never safe to rule out the possibility of a relapse. This, however, is not their main consideration ; their main consideration is that the court does not like to put such a prison sentence on the record of a young offender. Six months would look bad to a future employer, a passport authority ; six months would look very bad in a court. " We cannot change the law, sir, you must see that. We can only seek a reasonable solution."

The judge and his two dumb friends withdraw and when on their return they announce the reasonable solution, it sounds indeed a hybrid : Approved school, indeterminate period, two years deferment.

The girl grasps that if she is good she will be free to divide her time between the January cleaning and looking after the new baby.

" No more *Amerikaner*," says the prosecutor.

Munich: Summary Justice—A German Divorce

The father thanks the court. The girl says, " *Auf Wieder-sehn.*"

" We hope *not*," says the judge.

The next is an older mother accused of letting her daughter share her bed with *Them*. *Schwere Kuppelei*, they call the offence.

She is quite indignant. "She was engaged to the American gentlemen," she says. " Oh, yes, formally engaged, each time."

Big cases usually involve complex, many-stranded issues ; in small cases one too easily takes sides. If the judge is kind, intelligent and fair, and without that maddening streak of donnish-judicial remoteness from the facts of life, it is hard to sit in a court for any length of time without coming to look upon the people on the wrong side of the bar as so many oafs and morons. I had moreover taken against the inhabitants of Munich from the start, those Bavarian faces, that blend in the popular temper, one soon comes to feel, of frivolity and romanticism with simple brutality. I was spoken to by a number of people who told me admiringly how nice it was for England still to have the death penalty. And when in the North or in the Rhineland or in Baden they tell you how they never really took to Hitler, they never fail to point to Bavaria, his spiritual home, the breeding-ground and sanctuary of National Socialism. (In Bavaria, they tell you that the real Naziland was Saxony. Now cut off in the Eastern Zone.) So I was glad when I heard a case that shed a softer light.

Between assaulted minors, hefty girls who looked quite capable of holding their own at Buenos Aires, there appeared a mingy specimen of a man charged with house-breaking and illegal entry from Czechoslovakia. He had been in custody for some weeks (this was one of the speedy trials), and the policeman on the chair by him, sitting in his amplitude of flesh, looked of a different breed.

The facts were—none too quickly—told. The accused,

speaking poor German, inarticulate generally, was a Czech, twenty-eight years old and an unskilled worker; he had had enough and one night he walked across the border in the clothes he stood in hoping to reach Munich and there ask for asylum as a refugee. (I am also putting in this case because I heard a case similar in issue later on in Paris.)

Was he not aware, the Czech was asked, that he could have asked asylum at the first police station inside Germany?

He did not know, he thought he would have to go to Munich. He had been anxious to get as far as Munich.

Why had he not provided himself with *a little* money against his first needs? Had he not been in employment?

Oh, yes, he'd been working. He left on a Saturday evening, but he didn't take his Czech money. He thought it was better so.

After three days and nights in the Bavarian woods, he was worn out and hungry, his socks were walked to shreds. He broke into an empty week-end shack and there took, in the language of the charge sheet:

1 pair of worsted knee-socks	valued at	18s	4d
1 slab of chocolate	,,	1s	6d
1 package of pretzels	,,		11d
1 jar of honey	,,	5s	6d
1 package of 20 cigarettes	,,	3s	4d

What the Czech actually did was to wolf the chocolate and the pretzels, light a cigarette, find a spoon and eat about two thirds of the honey—it was all the food to be found—put on the clean socks, hang his own bloody rags over a chair, light another cigarette, put the package in his pocket, lie down on the couch and fall asleep. It was so that the Bavarian owner—who sat next to me during the trial uttering self-congratulatory noises—found him: in exhausted sleep, on the owner's couch, the owner's fine hand-knitted Bavarian knee-socks with tassels and embroidered tops on his legs, the jar of honey by his side with the spoon and the two stubs. The owner first woke him, then locked him in, then drove to fetch the police.

At the trial the Czech was not represented. He admitted all the facts. He put forward no defence.

" Are you an habitual smoker ? "

" Yes."

" How many a day ? "

" Forty."

The owner was asked if he wished to make a submission.

" *Yoah*," he said, " punishment."

The judge gave a sentence of four months, deferred ; and justified it as follows. The facts of the case themselves, he said, constituted a defence. House-breaking was a very serious crime, but here the question of guilt hinged on the question of Necessity, and in the view of the court there had been Necessity. The country between the Danube and the Czech border was wooded and lonely. The accused, for some obscure but well-lodged reason of his own, had been convinced that he must on no account appeal to an authority before reaching the capital ; he had been on the point of collapse from hunger and exhaustion. The taking of the articles of food was quite evidently covered by one legal definition of Necessity, *Mundraub* ; the taking of the knee-socks also—the police had testified as to the state of the man's own footwear— was covered by a definition of Necessity, *Notentwendung*. It was true that these socks happened to be far superior to the article they had served to substitute, but one had to bear in mind that these had been in fact the only pair of socks there was. The only doubt the court had had was over the package of cigarettes, the eighteen unsmoked cigarettes found in the accused man's pocket, but it was the opinion of this court that in the case of a man accustomed to smoking forty cigarettes a day, the taking of one packet must be considered provision for his journey and therefore Appropriation through Necessity rather than Theft.

The judge then asked the Czech whether he accepted the

judgment, and told him that in any case he was now free to go.

The man looked extremely worried.

"You must go to the Foreigners' Police," said the judge, "and get your status straightened out. If you like, the court will give you a letter."

I went behind the scenes to find out whether there was any chance of his being sent back to Czechoslovakia. He did not look, one must bear in mind, a very bright or healthy or useful addition to the Federal Republic. I was told that he certainly would not. Back in the corridor, I found the Czech encircled by a pressing mob—the audience from the public gallery. They had sent round the hat and were stuffing the proceeds into his pockets and limp hand.

—————————————

In the course of my first week in Munich I had happened to come in on the middle of a dullish case and had stayed to the end, fascinated by the manner of the judge, who looked like a young priest. On my last morning, wandering rather disconsolately about the passages—one does get very weary of it at times and there are days when it all looks stale and sad, pedantic, heartbreaking, stupid in the last analysis, and beside the point—, I decided to manage for myself a kind of farewell treat, I was going to hear that judge again. I did not know his name. The place is vast. I opened and shut doors, and when it did seem hopeless, went on with a kind of mechanical obstinacy. When I saw that very man hurry across a vestibule, I spoke to him on an impulse. I found it possible to tell him I had been impressed and why, and I asked him if he were sitting anywhere this morning might I come with him. At close quarters he did not look young. He still looked like a priest; a poor priest in a shabby soutane, with a worn youthful face. He was kind. He said to come but that he was afraid his second case was going to be a Matrimonial

Munich: Summary Justice—A German Divorce

Reconciliation, and all divorce proceedings had to be held in private. I said I knew that. He said to come anyway, and we would see.

He sat alone in what one might call chambers and which was a small bright room furnished like an office and equipped with a bright and pretty girl for shorthand-writer.

The first case was an application for reduction of alimony, and sheer heartbreak, something from the column of Miss Lonely-hearts. The wife, who was desperately resisting the reduction, was there, sitting with a flabby lawyer who had slipped in ten minutes late. The husband did not appear; his lawyer kept on adding figures in his brief as if he were trying to sort them out for the first time. It was evident from the start that the judge must have spent the night poring over them.

As the figures are going to recur I shall at once translate them into pounds.

Herr and Frau Kahn (I call them Kahn because that is not their name) were divorced some years ago. There were two young children. Frau Kahn was given custody, and Herr Kahn, who had just taken up a post as Government architect in the Rhineland with a salary of £800, was ordered to pay alimony of £250 a year. Meanwhile he had remarried and had had another child. At first the new wife had had a job, now she had fallen very ill. Herr Kahn could no longer manage to pay that slice out of his income.

Frau Kahn began by saying quietly that she did not believe a word of it. " You do not know my husband——"

The judge said that he realised from the correspondence that her husband had been very bad about the payments, he had been constantly in arrears long before his present difficulties began. " I do see that this was extremely hard on you and the children, but Frau Kahn, we cannot shut our eyes to the fact that we are now facing a radically changed situation. Unfortunately it is all quite true." The second wife, the poor young woman, had been struck by illness which had left her with a deformation of the spine, a permanent invalid. " I have the medical documents—they are at your disposal— it is an appalling thing really, and nothing can be done about it."

" I am very sorry about that," said Frau Kahn, who looked pretty tired herself.

" So now it is not only that she had to give up all thought of ever earning anything herself again, she is no longer able to do the housework for her husband and she cannot look after the child. The child has been boarded out, later on he will have to be sent to a boarding school and to holiday camps, all at great cost to your husband."

" There *are* institutions."

" *Frau Kahn*," says the judge.

" Yes, yes," she says, " I see."

" And therefore——"

" You can tell me what you like, but it isn't an excuse for my husband to wriggle out of his obligations. As he always has."

" An excuse, no. The question is how far *can* he now fulfil his obligations? All his obligations. We cannot ask people to do the impossible. I want you to realise how matters stand——"

" *I* do the impossible."

" And why ? "

" For my children of course. Herr Landrat, I love my children."

The judge says nothing.

" Quite—my husband, perhaps I should say ex-husband, wouldn't do it for *me*."

The judge says, almost *sotto voce*, " I worked out a little chart."

The lawyers come to life.

" It's just a note to help me, gentlemen. Your husband then, Frau Kahn, is earning £800 a year, you are earning just under £500 at your bank, is that right ? "

Munich: Summary Justice—A German Divorce

" It comes to exactly £493 a year."

" That is what I put down. So you see it is simply a question of dividing just under £1,300 between six people—three grown-ups, one of them an invalid, one of them in poor health—I do know that you, also, have been far from well—and three children. Here you are."

HUSBAND

Income	£800 a year	=	£16 a week
+ Alimony	£250	=	£5
Total Left	£550 a year	=	£11 a week for 2 Adults and 1 Child

WIFE

Income	£493 a year	=	£9 10 a week
− Alimony	£250	=	£5
Total Left	£743 a year	=	£14 10 a week for 1 Adult and 2 Children

" Herr Landrat, if you think you have proved now that that's a lot of money and that I get more than my husband, let me tell you . . . Fourteen pounds ten a week, you say, when my husband does pay up, which is not often and not without many efforts, letters, lawyers, running to offices in my luncheon hour—well, when we do get it, we can *just* manage, only just. Two growing children——"

" I do realise, Frau Kahn, I do——"

"—and I'm away from home all day, and I have to look fairly respectable at the bank, Herr Landrat, do you know the rent one has to pay if one doesn't want to bring up one's children in a barrack ? And I can't move further out, I couldn't leave them alone even longer than I have to now. Every penny, I tell you, goes into just keeping us going. You were right to say I was not well myself, I was in hospital again last August—ten days—I went home too soon. I've had this kidney thing ever since the boy was born. I shouldn't stand so much, it wears me out there are times when I think I cannot go on, I want to die. And it never stops. The housework, being in time for the office, getting back in time for the housework and their homework——"

The judge says, " I can see it all, Frau Kahn, and I do sympathize with you. But what can we do about it? You say —and I know it's true—you cannot afford any help on fourteen pounds ten a week, and your husband has eleven pounds a week and the domestic situation I told you about? "

" My husband could take on some extra work. I have to do work in the evening. I often stand and do the ironing and at the same time the little boy's arithmetic."

" Do you think your husband *would*? "

" Not a chance. Not he."

" You see we shall be forced to come to the decision to allow your husband some reduction."

" Herr Landrat, may I tell you the background story of this case? My husband and I were married in 1948. I was twenty-one and at the university, working for my degree. I was going to teach. My husband was twenty-two, he had just been demobilised and he wanted to become an architect. I broke off my studies and took a job as a telephone operator to make it possible. His training lasted for nearly six years, and all that time I stayed in that telephone exchange. I supported us all. I worked so hard that the little boy developed a nervous trouble because he was so much left alone as a baby, he is still under treatment now. Herr Landrat, one year after my husband got his diploma, he started having an affair with that girl. Six months later he left me for her."

The judge looked at her. " A very bad business."

" One more thing: If *I* had gone on with my degree, instead of financing my husband's, I should now have my own career, I always wanted to be a teacher, and I should be earning enough to keep my children and myself decently, and in security. My present job will lead to nothing, I had no training in banking, it was too late, I was only taken on as unskilled clerical staff. Now you have the whole situation. I never speak ill of their father to the children—nor to anyone—but sometimes one must speak out. . . ."

And so we heard that during the worst time after the war her husband had his shirts made to measure—when we couldn't afford a baby-sitter . . . "He is a selfish man, Herr Landrat," how he had always managed to get American cigarettes. "Is there no justice?"

"Would it be material——" said her lawyer, but the judge signed him to desist.

After some time, he said, "What do *you* suggest?"

She said, "He shouldn't be allowed to get away with it, and I really don't see how I can manage on less." Then she stiffened once more, "It's his moral obligation."

"We are here to decide on what is possible; now. We still have only £1,300 to divide between six people, and your husband has the heavier liabilities. And he is a civil servant, he, too, has to look fairly respectable at the ministry. We are obliged by law to leave a man enough not to impair his working capacity. Do you know what the prescribed legal minimum is for an unskilled, single working-man? £4. 10. 0. a week."

"Yes, but——"

"Frau Kahn, what do you think would happen if we refused this application of your husband's now?"

"He'd find some other way of getting out of paying."

"Like resigning his appointment and going into private practice and declaring a business loss?"

"He's quite capable of it."

"So it might be unwise—for *your* sake, Frau Kahn—to refuse this application?"

"Yes, but——"

"Herr Rechtsanwalt—do you think that if we allowed an

annual reduction of £50, which would bring the order down to £4 a week, your client would feel that his need had been met and would undertake to pay regularly ? "

" Yes, we would agree to that," says Herr Kahn's lawyer.

" Herr Rechtsanwalt—in the circumstances, would you consider this an acceptable solution for *your* client ? "

" I should recommend it," says Frau Kahn's lawyer.

" Frau Kahn—would you agree ? "

" Oh, very well," she says. " But——"

Presently the order is entered in due form.

When the shorthand writer has closed the protocol, and Frau Kahn gets up to go, the judge says to her, " This will not go on for ever. You know that your husband's salary is bound to rise. It looks as if he had a career in front of him, they'll probably make him *Oberbaumeister* in a few years. That would alter the circumstances. The courts would grant you an increase of order."

After she had left he said, " That was an unhappy story. There is so little we can do. All we can try is to heal; so often we succeed only in amputating. Was I wrong to hold out hope ? I made some inquiries—I'm not quite such a fool as I look—I think that man will rise. He is thought to have ability. *If* he is not crushed. That is another question : here we have a man who liked things easy, and now he has got two tragedies on his hands. She asked if there was no justice. I sometimes think there is too much."

Then he said, " Do smoke, please, if you wish. Oh, dear, we've over-run, I'm late again. The Reconciliation must be waiting." He explained that there can be no divorce without this hearing which is a formal invitation to reconsider and to make it up. Generally, they do not. " You had better stay. We shall have to ask the parties' permission."

Presently, a man and a woman enter, each with a lawyer. They sit down apart and without looking at each other. Both are middle-aged, both show traces of uncommon handsomeness, both are wooden-faced.

Munich: Summary Justice—A German Divorce

The judge begins by asking their consent for me to stay. The man shrugs and says, " Why not ? " The woman gives me one quick look, and says, " Yes." Her lawyer says, " I have no objection." The man's lawyer says, " English Press ? I don't think that would be at all desirable." I feel as if I were already guilty of having hawked his clients' private life to the Sunday papers. " This is of no interest," he says to me in a menacing tone. The judge puts my case, which makes me feel guilty in another way. " Oh, very well then," says the lawyer.

" Frau X., Herr X.—you have considered this : you are both now in your fifties—your children are married—you have been married yourselves for twenty-nine years—neither of you wishes, it appears, to set out on another marriage—have you asked yourselves whether it is worth breaking up your lives and your home at this stage ? " The grounds for this divorce are incompatibility and mutual consent. (Both are valid here.) " Could you think of burying your differences and going on as you were ? Herr X.——? "

The man chews his mouth. After a time he says ungraciously, " I wouldn't mind. She can stay. If she admits her guilt. [Suddenly colouring] If she *admits* it."

The woman says, " For nothing on earth."

There follows an outburst from the man. It is bitter, bitter. It is also savage and ranting and loud, yet all about petty things. The seed-cake she baked for the neighbours, the sugar and the egg *he* had walked twelve miles to find in 1946, the undone mending, the running to the cinema, " she never thinks of *me*, never of *me*, never——"

The woman says, " Herr Richter, a woman may be very guilty, a woman may feel very guilty, but no woman, Herr Richter, is able to live with having her guilt thrown in her face every day for sixteen years."

The man shouts a word ; then trembles.

The shorthand girl looks at the judge, pencil poised ? The judge lightly shakes his head.

" Herr X. are *you* quite blameless ? "

" I slept with every woman who came my way, I made all her friends. I did. I made her own sister. But that was afterwards. *Afterwards.* I didn't like it, it didn't help."

During the war something happened that could have happened to any woman. Here, ill luck, or circumstances, or fate, gave it an extra twist. And so something had to happen to the man that would be very hard for any man's pride, or fastidiousness, to bear. He came home on leave from the front in 1943, an N.C.O., possibly already a bit of a soft bully, his nerves shot to pieces. He learnt about his wife because he became ill. He never got over it. From that day on their life was hell.

When the spate of words and counter words was over, the judge dictated, " The parties, Herr X. and Frau X. of Y. appeared before me on this tenth day of November in the presence of the clerk and of (my name and address) and were duly invited to resume their marriage. The attempted reconciliation failed."

Their children are of age. " Maintenance ? "

" I want nothing," says the wife.

" That will make it all quite simple when your divorce comes up. That will probably be—not in December : the Christmas vacation—in January, in February more likely. It seems a pity . . . All the papers are ready. . . . To wait all that extra time. . . . The expense, too, having the case called a second time. It *is* a pity." The judge pulled his watch. " If only we had finished a bit earlier. A quarter past one, they're all gone now. You see, we have to be three High-court judges to pronounce a divorce. I wonder— There may still be someone in the building. Fräulein—? You think we might be able to find someone ? Ring down to Court VIII, will you ? "

Frau Landsgerichtsrat Holm has only just risen.

" Tell her to wait ! " cries the judge. " We shall be right down. Tell her we have a divorce. Come, follow me . . .

Munich: Summary Justice—A German Divorce

And you, come with me," grabbing my arm, robe flying, he is down the corridor. " No, not the lift, the lift is slow, I shall explain it all to you on our way down." We fly down the main staircase. Behind us is the shorthand writer, bearing the divorce file on her clipboard, behind her are the woman, and at some distance the husband and the panting lawyers.

Landsgerichtsrat Holm is disrobing, " Come with me, follow me—no, keep it on !—come quick, we have to find someone else, I'll explain it all to you as we go." We are trotting three abreast now. " Are they all there ? Are they following ? No, you stay here, it may interest you to see how things are done." Past cleaning women, past stray lawyers. " Can we go a little faster ? You don't mind, Frau Landrat ? I don't want them to wait all of those months, it wouldn't be at all good—— Let's try here."

The judge went out to luncheon half an hour ago, sir.

" Thank you. Come on, come on—we must try the other floor. And to pay all that money—— I must explain to you that here we have costs every time a case is called. Legal expenses are wicked. Frau Landrat, a little faster perhaps ? Here. No—locked. Come on, come on. . . ." We are frankly running ;

" Oh, dear no, that's the Amtsgericht wing, that's no use. Amtsgerichts judges cannot do a divorce. Half past one—we must hurry—this turning—are they following ? You must explain to me about procedure in England. Oh, here's a clerk—can you tell us, please ? No, I suppose not. *We cannot disappoint them now* . . . Where did you say ? Oberlandsgerichtsrat Staadler is working in his rooms ? Come along then ! Oh, no, Frau Landrat, he will be delighted. We must hurry. . . ."

Our cortege streams into the Appeal Court judge's rooms. He looks at us over his spectacles. " Really, Landrat, is this necessary ? "

" It is, it is. I'll explain it all to you as we go along. Put on your robes. We can stand, it won't take a minute. Are they all here ? "

The shorthand writer presents the file. The judge takes it, trying to get his breath. The Appeal-Court judge slings on his white tie. We group ourselves in a semi-circle. The judge gabbles through the pages as if he were conducting a Catholic country funeral. The parties look at the floor. As soon as the marriage is declared dissolved, the Appeal-Court judge disappears again into his inner room. The lawyers mark their briefs. A register is signed. There is some shaking of hands. The woman has already walked away. The man bows to the judge. And on this note of Alice directed by René Clair ended my encounter with the German legal system.

AN

AUSTRIAN

INTERLUDE

An Austrian Interlude

At the secretariat they thumbed my credentials with opaque, slow stares, loath to let go, loath to relinquish any scrap of paper, commit themselves to any response. I had seen it all before. In Portugal at the customs. In Mexico at the post office. In the East, in all those offices where print is new hard magic and responsibility is split among the underpaid to the last decimal. Here it is a legacy of the Hapsburg Empire, the mould of what was once regarded as the most senile bureaucracy of Europe, the spectre of the now amputated Balkans.

" The chief is not in."

Then someone came in about a key and everybody broke into recitative.

" Der Schlüssel ? "   " Nun sage ! "
" Wo ist er ? "   " Ich weiss nicht——"
" Wer hat ihn ? "   " Lasst hören——"
" Der Schlüssel ! "   " Der Schlüssel ? "
" Er hat ihn——"   " Nun weiter——"
" Doch kommt er——"   " Der Schlüssel ! "

When the key is found it unlocks a room like a class-room in a poor but decent elementary school. There is a smell of linoleum, chalk and people. On the wall hangs a large photograph, slightly warped, of the President of Austria, and a typed inventory of the furnishings which include a coat-rack and a spittoon. On the dais stand a crucifix and a candlestick with one candle.

This room remains empty for some ten minutes. Then a judge enters, followed by a kind of beadle. The judge is in a bit of a temper, though not seriously so.

" Where's die Fraülein ? "

" Don't know," says the beadle.

" Go and look ! "

" It's Tuesday."

" Tuesday ? "

Pause.

" Where are the files? Get me my files."

" Which ones ? "

[Shouting] " How should I know ? What are we doing ? Who's here ? "

" Nobody. We should have had the mo-peds at three o'clock."

" It isn't three o'clock," says the judge.

" No, sir."

[Pulling his watch. Shouting, but comfortable] " It is seventeen minutes past four."

" There are two advocates outside."

" Call them in."

" Yes, sir."

Two elderly legal gentlemen enter. They walk to the iron stove and rub their hands.

" *Servus*," says the judge. " Why don't we start ? "

1st Lawyer : " I am waiting for my witness."

2nd Lawyer : " A lad of sixteen ! "

1st Lawyer : " But a witness."

" Very *good* witnesses, lads of sixteen," the judge says to himself, dreamy but loud.

The beadle has returned. In his arms rests a large, new, shining portable typewriter. He sets it carefully on the judge's table.

" Take it away," says the judge.

An Austrian Interlude

The 2nd Lawyer says in a coaxing tone, " Perhaps we could have a look at the sketch ? "

" Which sketch ? "

" Of the accident."

" Well, where is your sketch."

" It's in the file."

" Oh."

" The sketch," the 2nd Lawyer says more firmly, " is worthless. Inadequate. Totally inadequate. What is more, it is misleading."

" Totally inadequate," says the 1st Lawyer, " *and* misleading."

The judge [examining his fingernails] : " Why should we look at a worthless sketch ? "

" I was hoping," says the 2nd Lawyer, " I was going to respectfully request the court to order the Comandatur to draw us another one."

" Very well, we're going to tell them to draw us another sketch, an adequate sketch. A totally adequate sketch. Where's die Fräulein——? [To the beadle] Remind me to tell her to make out an order to the Comandatur."

The beadle says, " Bezirks-Leutenant Paschenko drew that sketch."

" Oh, he," says the judge. " He's going to retire. They'll pension him off. The Bezirks-Leutenant—he's going. Very well then, gentlemen, that'll be all for today. There *isn't* anything else ? Well *servus*, gentlemen." His eye falls on me.

" Do you *want* anything ? "

I explain that I have to come to study the Austrian legal system.

" *Jeezus*," says the judge.

————————————

Altogether I only spent one week in Austria (five court days) in two places which shall be nameless. One of them had

An Austrian Interlude

a Bezirksgericht, a court of petty-sessional level; the other, a provincial capital, had a high court as well, but it was not sitting. I did not go to Vienna. So what I met in the course of this excursion is no more—and no less—representative of Austrian justice than two days, say, with the Justices at Great Dunmow, Essex, and three at Bristol Quarter Sessions would be of English justice as a whole.

In large outline the Austrian system, on paper, is much like the German. In detail, there are many variations in penalties and procedure. One might regard it as one does the language —to English ears it is one foreign language and the differences are hardly worth discerning, whereas to the Austrians and Germans they are important and distinct. There is, for example, the jury system: In Germany, as we have seen, the jury deliberates with the bench and decides on sentence as well as guilt. In Austria, the jury begins by deliberating alone and in secret on the question of guilt, then after eventual conviction joins the bench to deliberate on sentence.

Historically, Austria, like Prussia and unlike the Southern German states, was late in liberalizing its penal system. While the Prussian system had been in the main politically oppressive, the Austrian was also signally brutal in its dealings with common criminals. The use of heavy chains in prisons, for instance, was only abolished in the nineteen hundreds. During the *Anschluss* years, Austria retained its own codes and procedure, subject to the usual Nazi changes. And here, also, the Nazi changes were thrown out after the war; and like Germany, Austria abolished capital punishment in 1949.

A really filthy bunch stood before the bench. The woman in carpet-thick petticoats and matted gipsy hair, the men in broken shoes, their trousers held up by string.

" Ah," cries the judge, "the cabbage case!" (It is our friend of yesterday.) " What did you steal?"

178

An Austrian Interlude

" Cauliflower."

" *Good*," says the judge. " Let's have the witnesses."

" One witness," says the clerk.

" *Excellent*. Call him in."

It is a woman.

" Name—born—place—married or single—religion ? "

" Catholic."

The clerk lights the candle on the dais.

" Put it out," says the judge.

" The oath, sir."

" We're not going to take an *oath*. Where do you think you are ? Assizes ? [To the witness] So they took the cauliflower."

" I was standing in my garden, sir——"

" Make it short," says the judge.

" They came on a motor-scooter, the woman held the sack——"

" That's not true," cry the accused.

" *Ruhe !* " cries the judge.

The public prosecutor stands up and says, " Venerable Court, I submit punishment for the accused." Not a word more, not a word less.

" Excellent," says the judge. He gets to his feet at once. " Three days each for the cabbage thieves." He has wasted no breath on Hans Karl Georg Joseph Maria Schmied. The accused shrug and smirk.

One man stammers something about how pleased he is it's so little, thank you, and when should they start ? Notification, says the judge. Meanwhile the other two have rallied and start a chorus about loss of work, your Excellency, what about compensation for the day and bus fare for the bus ?

" None of that," says the judge. " *Basta*."

I step up to ask if he has finished for the day.

" One's never finished," the judge says with a yawn.

" Anything *on* ? "

" Oh, plenty, plenty. *You* sound like a German."

The clerk volunteers that there will be a case before a limited jury in the afternoon.

" Holy souls in heaven," says the judge, " so there is. *Gnädige, I' küss die Hand.*"

The serious young Swiss, who has come to stand his trial for manslaughter, looks drawn. The trial begins thirty-five minutes late. The public prosecutor stumbles through a prepared script. A year and six months ago, a boy on a motor-scooter was killed at a crossroads. The Swiss had been driving along a main road at cruising speed, saw the crossing, saw the side road, saw that it was marked off by white lines, assumed priority, carried on. The boy on the scooter crossed the white lines at a good speed: collision; death. The Swiss, as it turned out, had not had priority, there had been no corresponding sign on the main road, the white lines across the side road were a meaningless mistake, the local boy who crossed them knew it.

Defence counsel rose to say that his client had asked him to express his deep regret to the court. Whoever was to blame, a young man near his own age had lost his life and his client was acutely conscious of that fact. He wished——

" We'll take it as heard," says the judge.

The lawyer—a good lawyer—presents the defendant's case. The judge takes out his watch. His client had made an error, the lawyer says, a fatal error, but a justifiable one. He would call a traffic expert. The expert is not brief, it is a knotty problem. Throughout, the judge stares at his watch. The public prosecutor, who looks like a poor monkey, crouches behind his desk, frowning vacantly.

The two jurors began by being more alert, but soon succumb to the form.

All the same, one of them insists on a question, Was anything done about the white lines?

"Was anything done about the white lines?" asks the judge, looking round.

"The white lines have been removed since, sir," says the clerk.

"Satisfied?" says the judge.

"I submit punishment for the accused," says the public prosecutor. Feeling that something more may be needed, he adds, "Exemplary punishment."

The judge eyes him mercilessly. "The gentlemen of the jury are entitled to hear your argument."

The prosecutor draws a breath. "The white lines," he says, "the white lines were a nonsense. They were an unreason, they meant nothing. . . ." Soon he is in a lather. "Anyone, anyone I tell you, any malefactor, any criminal, any—well, any person, could scrawl white lines across a road! Where would we be—where would we be indeed—if it became lawful—if it became all right—for people to pay attention—to pay attention to those white lines—if people scrawled white lines—across roads—across public roads—it would be chaos, gentlemen, catastrophe!—muddle——"

"*Very* good," says the judge.

And during the whole of the closing speech for the defence, he not only stares, but drums.

While the judge and jury are out, the Swiss and his lawyer walk the corridor. To the eternal question, will they be long? the clerk replies darkly, "*He* never comes back before five."

And when the whole court is standing ready to deliver, and to hear, sentence, there is a last delay. The public prosecutor. He slips in after a minute. I can see that in his cupped hand, under his gown, he is holding a lighted cigarette. The judge begins—conviction; three months' prison; deferment for three years; restitution of passport; costs. The prosecutor has managed to stub out the cigarette on his shoe. He puts the stub into a little tin. The lawyer leads the Swiss away.

——————————————

A woman is brought before the court (after a night's rest) on a charge of malicious damage.

" A *curtain*," says the judge. " You would think that people might use thread and needle. Married—occupation—religion ? "

" Protestant."

The judge is jolted into attention. " Write it down," he says.

" The curtain," says the protestant woman, " was deliberately hung up on our side of the passage. I had every right to take it down."

The judge has penetrated into the file. " *Tore* it down,"

" Under provocation. My daughter will tell you——"

" What's the daughter got to do with it ? "

" My daughter is a witness——"

" Oh, call her in. What's her name ? "

" Heiltrud."

" *Heiltrud*," says the judge, and plunges in his file. " Born in 1939! Heiltrud *was* a name in 1939."

The poor girl says her piece.

" Herr Staatsanwalt ? "

The prosecutor barks up, " I submit punishment for the accused."

" Etcetera amen," says the judge. " Thirty schillings fine. We have [dragging every word] a co-ordinated issue in this case, the injured party wants compensation."

" I submit compensation for the injured party," says the prosecutor.

" *Papagei*," says the judge. " How much ? We want to know *how much* ? Come on, tell us—what's the damage ? "

An Austrian Interlude

Nobody knows. The clerk says he's heard the curtain has been mended. Someone *has* used a thread and needle.

The judge tosses his biretta into the air. "Adjourned! Get the gendarmerie to go and have a look at it. [In profound disgust] Case adjourned for assessment of damage." He picks up his papers. "Heiltrud," he says as he marches out, "Heiltrud."

The prosecutor immediately lit a half of a cigarette. "Did you get that?" he said. "A *Protestantin*."

"She comes from Outside," said the clerk. Outside is the time-honoured Austrian word for Germany. "She says she is a widow, you know what they say she really is?" The clerk drew nearer, "they says she is—d i v o r c e d ."

PART THREE

SWITZERLAND

I

Schaffhausen—An Introduction

Perhaps I should make it clear—a writer ought sometimes to lay his prejudices on the table—that what I was looking for in all those law courts was for the best one could do. Within our limitations, and given reasonably good social and political circumstances. Contact with the law, intrinsically, is harsh enough and heaven knows that there are many, many ways of doing injustice. So I had and have no desire to visit the courts of countries behind the iron curtain, of Portugal or of Spain. For the rest the choice made itself. France was inevitable, France is still Europe. Germany had just crossed a rubicon. The United States, much to my regret, were impossible for practical reasons. I should very much indeed have liked to go to Holland and to one or all of the Scandinavian countries, particularly to Denmark, but unfortunately I speak neither Dutch nor Danish, Swedish nor Norwegian, which ruled that project out. The only accessible of the " good " countries then was Switzerland, and there I went with expectations and alacrity.

I went first to the patrician town of Schaffhausen and there fell in at once with a learned clerk of the Ober-Kantonalgericht, which is the State Court of Appeal. (Clerks, in this the oldest democracy of the Western Hemisphere, are lawyers of high standing who may well end up on the bench of the Supreme Court, while judges, high-court judges, need not have read law—it is but the English idea of lay justices carried a step further.) He handed me a nicely printed copy of the Cantonal Statute of Procedure and asked what had made me choose Schaffhausen.

I told him that one must begin somewhere, and that I had been to this agreeable place before and liked it.

My new protector pondered this. Their judicature here, he conceded, was *soigné*. They must see to it that I was given a good start; there was luckily a highly interesting law case coming up, a dispute about a labour contract—he was warming —*hoch intéressant.*

When ? I asked.

On Thursday before the Court of Appeal at half past one in the afternoon. He looked doubtful. That would give me a bare four days to make myself acquainted with the facts. It was about this employer on the one hand, he had engaged a workman ; now they'd made a curious contract—— He broke off. " I mustn't spoil it." He bade me come to his office presently after lunch. The file this minute was with the president. A shame my wasting nearly a whole half-morning, would I—perhaps ?—like to hear an actual case ? It might not be wholly uninstructive. *In medias res ?* As it happened, there was a case on to-day. Schuldhafter Ungehorsam, Culpable Disobedience, Kleinjustiz, a summary matter, generally dealt with by the organs of the Communal Police, unless the defendant wished to dispute the facts. That would start me from the bottom. So if I really felt up to plunging in, his Waibel would take care of me.

The Waibel—I had half expected to see my learned acquaintance's wife—was a portly, middle-aged personage in undertaker's clothes hung with a silver chain who took me to a seat. I felt I might as well have gone to Norway. He told me in a stage hiss, who was who.

"Down it came, crashing right in front of my feet," said the woman who was a witness.

"We are grateful for that piece of good fortune. Did you see it fall ? "

Schaffhausen: An Introduction

"Yawa. T'cat."

"Did you see t'cat push it or tumble it, Frau Witness?" said the judge. "What did t'cat do?"

"Jchump."

"*After* the fall?"

"Yawa. T'cat was scared. Pot crashed to pieces on the pavement, earth and all."

"Now listen, Frau Witness, the Herr Zinder here says it was not his cat?"

"Nanei, that'sh truth, it'sh t'harnessmaker's cat, she always sits in that window this time of year."

"Herr Polizei Representative would you like to make some comment?"

"Well, Herr Gemeinderichter, it's like this. It may have been t'cat. It may not have been t'cat. What interests us is the undisputed fact that the flower-pot fell into the street. And that means that the flower-pot was not secured to the window-sill according to the *règlement*."

"Herr Zinder, what have you got to say to that?"

All of this has been conducted in the language called Schwyzerdütsch, and the defendant's answer sounded something like, "Yawa, d'frue hatchs mi s'dreightly g'moa," which conveyed that the wife had used a bit of wire.

"*Malheureusement*," said the judge, "it was not *suffisant*."

"Well then, to the *Leumund*: you haven't got anything else on your conscience, Herr Zinder?"

"Nanei. Everything in order."

Leumund is an old-fashioned word meaning reputation, more than reputation: moral and material status.

"D'Leumund ish guet," said the Police Representative pleasantly, handing up some papers.

The judge fished for his spectacles. [Reading aloud] "'The neighbourhood is unanimous that Herr and Frau Zinder are a righteous, order-loving couple in well-regulated circumstances. Their house is always clean. The young wife is amiable and helpful to everyone. They are fond of going out

of an evening, but they owe nowhere.' And who's the other
one from, Herr Polizeivertreter ? "

" T'supérieur where he works."

" ' Herr Zinder is known to me as a good and honourable
bureau employee. He is punctual and industrious. He is not
always quite as careful as he might be and on Saturdays he is
often in a bit of a hurry to get away to go to the inn, but that
can be ascribed to his lack of years. He gets on well with his
fellow workers.' " The judge hands back the papers.
" D'Leumund ish guet."

" Yawyawa," says the Police Representative.

" Herr Zinder," says the judge, " listen to me a-while.
It's like this. You might say, it's not a great crime, it's just
a carelessness, a thoughtlessness, an oversight. You meant
no harm, and furthermore it was the wife who saw to tying
up the flower-pots. And that's true enough, Herr Zinder,
but that's not the half of it. It's carelessness and little
oversights that cause the great *malheurs*. You can praise the
Lord in Heaven, and so can the Frau Witness, that no harm
came of it this time. Think of the fearful danger in our streets
if geranium pots came crashing down on people's heads ! "

It is no idle threat. All windows in those handsome Swiss
towns sport flowering pots and boxes, in fact in many places
the inhabitants are held by law to decorate their casements,
and some townships go so far as to prescribe the colour and
the species, generally red geraniums, and for once the results of
interference with the subjects' liberty are at least very pretty.

" T'règlement, Herr Zinder, is not made to chicane the
citizen. It's to keep down the hazards of life. You disobeyed
t'règlement. You say it was your wife's duty, it was your duty
to see that she carried it out. You are the master of your home,
Herr Zinder. It is understandable for a young husband not to
be wanting to look over his wife's shoulder all the time,
have you done this ? Are you going to do that ? but that's the
way the law sees it, Herr Zinder. You are the householder,
you are responsible. Is that clear to you now ? "

Schaffhausen: An Introduction

"Yawa shoah," says the defendant.

"So *malheureusement*, considering the gravity of the risk, we must impose the fine."

The Police Representative concurs. They call it by another old-fashioned word, *Busse*, a penance. Thirty Swiss francs, then. And costs, say the police, a writing fee of one franc seventy-five centimes, and that was all. The summons had been taken round by hand.

"And five francs litigation tax," says the judge. "The defendant is held to secure his geranium pots. Herr Zinder, no more bits of wire?"

"Nanei," he says. "So then—adieu alle mit'einand."

The Waibel leaves my side to get his stocking purse; it is full of coin, and he is paid in cash at once.

After lunch, in that part of the world, is half past twelve. Herr Dr. K. had not been idle. In his secretary's office, a table was laid for me with *Literatur*. I sat down to statutes, commentaries, files, balanced in neat stacks.

Dr. K. had asked me where was *descendue*? was the hotel all right? The question was put partly out of genuine concern and partly, I realised, out of interest in my *Leumund*. I happened to have gone—pure chance—to the Evangelical Hostel, which besides its more ostentatious virtues also had the ones of offering solid comforts and of being quite expensive, so I came out of it pretty well.

The secretary was a lean and elderly person dressed in black overalls with a tight bun of greying hair, who seemed cast for the part of a Victorian village schoolmistress, until she opened her mouth when a more bonhominous Swiss note came in. She switched on a green-shaded lamp. I opened a few books.

My host, like a St. Bernard, eager, helpful, but not fast, kept on bringing more.

Switzerland

" Schurter & Fritzsche [2 Vols] on Civil Litigation, highly *intéressant*, and here's Stämpfli on Federal Law, also highly *intéressant*," he stood over me as I lifted the covers, " and these are our own reports . . ."

I opened *Annual Report by the Cantonal High Court to the Parliamentary Grand Council of Schaffhausen for the Year* 1958. In arrangement and format, though bulkier, it resembled a Home Office Research Unit Report. On the editorial page, I saw my host's name.

" I brought along the volumes for 1938, 1928, 1918 and 1908," he said.

Each contained a complete account of business, civil, criminal, financial and administrative, transacted by the courts during the given year, broken down and cross-referred statistically every correlated which-way—substance, quantity, relation, time and place. It covered everything from complaints received to decisions reversed on appeal. There were tables listing warrants, inquests, remands, searches, hearings ; tables dealing with successions, legal aid, missing persons, licensed fire-arms, bankruptcy and recovered debt ; tables on expenditure ; tables showing how many persons had been detained for how many days and why, tables classifying offences by offences, and others by offenders' occupation, residence, sex and age ; tables establishing the ratio between convictions and acquittals, between sentences served and sentences deferred, and a table showing how many litigants had sued for what and how many had been successful and how long it had taken and how much it had cost whom.

" We do one every year," said Dr. K.

I expressed admiration.

He agreed that such reports were useful as well as interesting, they did give one a continuous picture. Theirs, of course, was only a small and mainly rural Canton, presently he would fetch last year's Zurich—the Zurich court reports had been coming out uninterruptedly since 1831.

" Monuments of labour."

Schaffhausen: An Introduction

" It's the law," he said. " The reports must go to parliament every year."

" Do they read them ? "

" Every report is examined by a parliamentary commission. Afterwards we have a full debate. The controversial points are usually about delays and costs. If they're not satisfied with the way the courts are run, they'll criticise and make recommendations."

" How about judicial independence ? "

" It's like this," said Dr. K. Judicially, the courts are independent, neither parliament nor the government can interfere with a judgment. Swiss courts, however, are also part of the administration, they administer themselves and are generally in charge of the entire judicial administration of a Canton, and as such they are controlled by the people.

Control by the people has a hollow ring. In the dinosaur countries, swamped by urban and suburban masses, hamstrung by a two-party system, such democratic statements are shabby lip-service, in Switzerland they bear some relation to reality. The government is not centralised, and even the whole Federation is still small enough—four and a half million people—to be a graspable community. Direct, small-scale democracy has been the citizens' conscious practice for some six hundred and fifty years. Week in week out, the voting population is on the run to the urns to decide, not on a limited choice of intermediaries or a package policy, but on this or that specific issue, often raised by a private member of the electorate itself. There is a flourishing provision called the Initiative by which anybody with the required number of signatures can put anything to the local or the national vote, and the required number for a referendum on federal level, is only thirty thousand.

" Do you still put nearly all of your legislation to the general vote ? " I asked, " and is it not expensive and slow, and are people really willing to digest all those bills ? "

Expensive, he conceded. There were the printing costs,

high but necessary. Slow, he waved aside. The rest was a matter of drafting—a bill had got to be concise and clear. As a lawyer, he saw in that both loss and gain. Some laws were all too bluntly worded, and yet this gave the judges much discretionary scope.

" And who," I said, " appoints the judges ? "

" *Elects.* The judges are elected." By direct vote in the smaller Cantons ; by parliamentary deputies in others. Never for life. For a term. The qualifications for a judgeship of the Federal Court are the same as those for a Member of Parliament, he must be a Swiss citizen and over twenty years old. He cannot be a woman. He cannot be clergy. He need not be a lawyer. For the Cantonal judgeships the qualifications vary, except that everywhere a judge must be male and Swiss. If he is elected he serves his term, and when the term is up he must stand for re-election.

There, I said, I found an order of things difficult to accept.

" Our judges are not the servants of a *crown*," said Dr. K.

" They are the *servants* of the people."

" The representatives."

I spoke of the political element, and of insecurity.

Dr. K. said that I was making a false analogy with the United States, the Swiss judicial elections were not political in the American sense ; they might be said to cut across party lines and personal ambition, and the results were generally determined by experience and common sense. The best man won.

" You are fortunate."

The system, he said, could only be appreciated in connection with Swiss history and traditions.

" And Swiss civic maturity."

Dr. K. shrugged. " It is far from ideal. *We* always think the English are so disciplined. Well, yes, perhaps on the whole we have been lucky."

" A judgeship for a term. One *could* get used to the idea . . . Perhaps it *is* a good idea—an excellent idea. As long as a man would not have to rule his conduct on the bench with an eye to re-election. A judge could go back to some other job like an M.P. The more one thinks of it, the more one likes it. We think of our judges as men of ninety and above the common law. Are your terms *long*? "

" It may be eight years, or five ; in some places it's only three. It varies from Canton to Canton."

" There are," I said, " twenty-two Cantons ? "

" Twenty-five. Nineteen Cantons and six Half-Cantons."

" Three are doubles ? "

" Halves. Two singles. Three are two. Two each."

" Split, like identical twins ? or different ? "

" Independent," said Dr. K. " Independent *Half-Cantons*."

" Of whom ? The other half ? "

Dr. K. was beginning to find me slow. " Yawyaw, *certainement*, own constitution, own legal system."

" Making their own independent annual report to parliament ? "

" Cantonal Parliament."

Something now entirely dawned on me. " *Twenty-five* independent Swiss Cantonal Legal Systems—*different* systems?"

" Yawyaw."

" Schaffhausen, then, is a law unto itself ? " I took in the pile of literature in front of me. " The system of Schaffhausen is unique ? "

My host nodded modestly.

" Ah well, like the United States. The law of the sovereign Commonwealth of Massachusetts, the law of California——"

Not like the United States. The law, contrariwise, was now federal law. " We scrapped the Cantonal Civil Codes, and in 1912 we adopted a Common Civil Code for the whole of the Federation." And thirty years later on it was decided—by popular referendum—to do the same with criminal law, and the first unified Swiss Criminal Code was established (by a narrow majority) in 1942. Yet the application of these common codes is still left entirely to the individual Cantons. Here they act as they choose. They organise the courts according to their own rules, they legislate their own procedure.

" You mean," I said, " you mean that Lucerne may try by jury whereas Appenzell does an identical case before a bench of five judges, and Solothurn of three, and Geneva rules out evidence that would be perfectly admissible at Berne ? "

" Yawyaw."

Did it not enormously confuse and complicate things ? Was there any present trend towards uniformity ?

Dr. K. did not think there was. Procedure, it had indeed been found, tended to date fairly quickly nowadays, and during the last century the Cantons had changed or over-hauled their various codes of procedure on the average every thirty years, but it was usually a change in line with their local idiosyncrasies and needs.

I remarked on the formidable volume of technicalities a lawyer would have to master before he could practise ; or need he be familiar only with the rules of his own Canton ? Dr. K. answered cryptically that these days it was more or less accepted that lawyers could not be entirely eliminated from the courts.

I said that had been my impression.

" Elsewhere," said Dr. K., " lawyers are respected. Here we have a prejudice against them." Not as in France and Germany where qualified representation is compulsory in some of the higher courts, no-one in Switzerland need ever employ a barrister ; as in England, he may appear for himself. (Not as in England), he may also choose to be represented by any person of his choice, a friend, an uncle, an expert or a colleague. These occasional pleaders usually have to preserve their amateur status, yet in some small Cantons laymen—of good moral repute—are admitted to regular and gainful practice at the bar.

" Are there no bar examinations of the habitual kind ? "

" Some Cantons exact them."

Schaffhausen: An Introduction

" In the others it goes by *Leumund* ? "

" S'il vous plait ? "

" But the litigants and the bench are satisfied ? It works ? "

" Yawyaw."

Presently Dr. K.'s secretary recalled him to sterner duties.
I was left alone with her and the law books. Her name, I had
learnt, was Frau Hirt. She put another file on my table, then
went herself to a resplendent typewriter that looked as
streamlined and up-to-date as she was not. These balanced,
happy people, I thought with pleasure, have got the secret of
using the new techniques and remaining their own selves.

" So you will be spending the whole of your first year
with us ? " she remarked and settled down to her task.

I addressed myself to mine. It was going to be simple
after all. I could not begin to try to study the twenty-five
Swiss legal systems ; I would try to look at the common
denominator.

II

Schaffhausen—A Law Case

The great day came. Professionals generally seem to feel concern that their guests in court will be bored stiff, and in England little except libel and the more eccentric forms of fraud are deemed to be tolerable entertainment ; the French express regret when they cannot produce a murder, Si vous étiez venu le jour du type qui a zigouillé ses bonne femmes. Dr. K. was as happy as a man taking a boy to his first circus.

We were drinking coffee together just before the hearing. Was I sure I had the facts, and had I brought his plan ? He had drawn a plan of the seating of the five Appeal Judges. " The one to the left of our Chairman is a master printer, he has his own works." The one at the end was a mayor, a socialist and a labour councillor. On the right was the Vice-Chairman of the court, an industrial entrepreneur and a jurist. Was I sure I would understand ? The bench to-day would speak High German and not dialect as this was the tradition of the Court of Appeal. It would not extend to the parties ; the original Plaintiff would be represented by someone from his Trade Union. The Defendant would appear for himself. Both sides had appealed. " Oh, I wonder how we are going to decide to-day. I wonder how we ought to decide, it is such a curious case."

It was not only kindness and care itself, it was also infectious. It sprang, one felt, from a satisfaction with life and a man's

Schaffhausen: A Law Case

work in it and the sense that things ran well in a possible world and could be made to run perfectly.

The Schaffhausen Courts have a house in Herren-Acker, a calm and spacious square. We parted at the doors. It is not the Swiss custom for judges to come on. They make a private entrance, settle down, and when they are ready, parties and the public are called into the court.

It was a well-shaped room. The judges, dressed in everyday clothes, sit in a row of separate desks. As in Germany, there are no national, heraldic or religious emblems. There is no policeman. Dr. K. has a large desk, there are two upright ones for the litigants, a seat for the usher and few chairs for press and public. Both were absent.

The style of address is Herr President for the Chairman, and Herr Oberrichter for the other judges. Dr. K. is Herr Obergerichtsschreiber.

And this was the case under appeal. It was all too decidedly not a fascinating one to the general public, though to the *aficionado* it had its points. The Defendant, a contractor, had secured the services of the Plaintiff, a young workman skilled in a special line of metal work. The young man was trained as what they called a *Schabber* and there was never any doubt as to his exquisite ability.

" He does a beautiful piece of *schabbing*," witnesses had said in the lower court.

The contractor had made an agreement with this workman which guaranteed him full employment at the current rate of pay, which for this sort of job was 4.80 francs Swiss or 8/- an hour, that is £18 for a forty-five hour week. After a time the contractor failed to procure work. The workman remained idle for three weeks, after which he became discouraged with waiting and took a job elsewhere. Meanwhile he had not been paid and, under his agreement, claimed his wages. The contractor did not pay. The workman sued.

The Defendant's defence was (a) that the workman was not

entitled to draw pay automatically but only if he failed to find work elsewhere; (b) that the employer was in any case only liable for the sum wanted to make up the difference between unemployment assistance and the full wage. The workman had sat back and neither looked for work nor applied for assistance.

The workman had contended as to (a) that he *had* tried to find other work; as to (b) that given the agreement he had neither felt obliged nor entitled to seek unemployment assistance.

The lower court had held that there were two issues, an interpretation of contract: was the workman entitled to automatic pay or was he obliged to make some efforts of his own? And if he was so obliged, had he made such efforts? The court had raised the issues but had not pronounced on them, and instead come to a decision that was something of a compromise. It found for the Plaintiff and awarded him two weeks' wages, fifty francs compensation for litigation and two thirds of his costs.

The Defendant had appealed. The Plaintiff had also appealed, wanting his full three weeks' wages plus interest and the whole of his costs.

There is an undercurrent to the case. The contractor was not a contractor in the metal line at all, but a pastry-cook who was trying to get rich quick by securing the services of some highly skilled workmen and hiring them out at a profit. The venture had not been successful and the poor man was now beset with many difficulties. The abducted workmen had all been trained at the expense of a large metal works, and there was resentment in several quarters.

The most interesting feature of some Swiss appeal cases, as Dr. K. had pointed out, was the principle of open court at all stages; the judges deliberate, and put their final decision to the vote, in public. This is the practice of the Federal Court, followed by some Cantonal Courts, who hold that it is desirable for litigants and public to follow every step in reasoning and motivation whatever the cost might be in flexibility and freedom of debate.

First, the workman's case was put by his representative, the man from the Trade Union. He read, in Schwyzerdütch, a longish prepared statement. It was turgid, somewhere containing the expected gist, and very dull. He made one sensible point : the young man had had no wish to hang about in idleness, it was his employer who had begged him not to quit, new work was waiting round the corner.

The Defendant, the middle-aged pastry-cook, spoke freely, but added nothing to the argument.

" Yaw-shoah, I've nothing against the lad. He was *obstiné* about the Assistance. I had to appeal, Herr President, because I cannot pay."

The judge who was the socialist and country mayor, spoke first. He was a youngish man and his mind moved fairly quickly ; he spoke slowly though, making sure that he was followed. It's like this, he said, he had no doubt that the Defendant's appeal should be dismissed. The agreement might be unusual but it meant exactly what it said—a guarantee against loss of wages. Considering the Defendant's venture, a loss of wages was not only possible, it was highly probable. They must both have known perfectly well that without precisely this agreement the Defendant could not have secured the Plaintiff's services at all. The agreement had been the *sine qua non.* Then what happened ? The new contractor had managed to secure a couple of construction jobs and at first all went well. The jobs came to an end, new ones were slow in forthcoming and one fine Monday morning there was no more work. Did anyone *sérieusememt* expect the young Plaintiff to have walked out then and there to look for work elsewhere ? And at the end of that week the Defendant had not paid him, nor had he given him notice—there was no time limit in the agreement—he just told him to go on waiting in the hope of some new work. It was of course vital for the contractor that the workman should stay on ; without skilled labour at his instant service, all his hopes of future work collapsed. By keeping the workman on, he took a calculated risk, and so the pay promised in the agreement must be regarded as being in the nature of a retainer and as such it was due in any circumstance.

On the other hand, the judge said, taking it all in all, the lower court decision to award only two weeks' wages had not been unjust. After two weeks of waiting with no pay, common experience ought to have told the young man to clear out. So, although he was not too happy about the Plaintiff's having to bear a part of the costs, he was inclined to think that his appeal, as well, should be dismissed.

The next judge to give his opinion was the Vice-Chairman, a white-haired lawyer, and here the case received a check. He said he disagreed with his confrère. He was prepared to argue that the agreement could not be interpreted as guaranteeing automatic pay, and so the wages could not be said to have been due in any circumstances, and if one accepted that premise then all circumstances of the case became material and therefore one had to consider a point which had been raised, namely should or could the Plaintiff have claimed unemployment benefits. Personally, he was *douteux* whether it was possible to draw public assistance in order to ease a third party's obligation under a private contract, but he felt that the court should take this case no further until they had cleared up this point.

All looked at the Chairman. He was a full-time judge and a Member of Parliament at Berne. "Well, *bien——*?" he said.

A fourth judge, the master printer, spoke with ponderous energy. He agreed that the contract was not all cut-and-dried, he did not like the contract at all and he was prepared to argue on that aspect of the matter, and he did not think the question of unemployment benefits came into it at all. Unemployment benefits were a red herring, and it was preposterous to imagine that Cantonal Assistance would have paid a centime piece. . . .

Schaffhausen: A Law Case

The fifth judge said, "*Clairement*, if a man is under contract he is employed, whether he does actual work or not. *Contrairement* if the contract is not right——"

Here the workman's representative raised his arm, he had with him a ministerial directive on unemployment benefits, might he read it?

"Herr Läberli," said the Chairman, "an administrative directive is not binding on this court, but perhaps it might be a help to hear it."

It was worded in a way to leave the question much as it had been before.

The Vice-Chairman said, nanei, they had better look up some decisions of the Trade Supreme Court or refer to Berne. Dr. K. cut in to suggest putting the case as it was to the local Assistance office and ask them what they would have done.

The judge who was a mayor said, "A very good idea, Herr Doktor."

The Chairman looked as if he wished to speak and they all turned to him. "It's like this," he said. To him the case was clear—the Plaintiff was under no real obligation to look for assistance or other work, and so one might safely drop the unemployment benefits question. *Maintenant*, as some of the confrères did not hold his view of the main issue, it would be right to make sure of every subordinate point. Herren Oberrichter——

"Is it going to cost more?" asked the Defendant.

"Yaw-shoah."

So it was put to the vote; the five were unanimous to seek certainty and the case was adjourned *sine die*.

Dr. K., after all, was to get his wish. I did hear a rounded case in his Canton. That very evening a theft took place at Schaffhausen. The thief, caught red-handed by the jeweller's wife, was near penniless and a stranger, so they put him in the rose-walled jail next to the museum, and it was decided to have him tried with all dispatch. On the Monday following the Criminal High Court convened with a bench of three.

The Waibel introduced, " Signore Arrigo Bellini," and there entered a handsome, desperate, young Italian, dark and curled, for all the world to look at like the young Lord Byron.

It is the pride and self-imposed duty of Swiss judges to be able to conduct a hearing in any one of the four national languages.

The Chairman, a whole-time judge with an appearance of extreme distinction, put forth carefully, "D o v e s i e t e n a t o ?" It was adequate in all but accent ; like an English judge's Latin it sounded local and academic rather than Latin and living.

The fellow flung himself into position. "A Mantova, Signore ! "

"S c u o l a ?" As in Germany, the initial stage of a trial is concerned with the accused's past and person.

A shrug of hands. " Sette anni."

"L a v o r a t e ? "

" Fatto il mecanico." He's worked in Francia, he's worked with la Citroën, now he's come to Svizzera.

They run into a bit of trouble over the previous convictions. The Chairman is obliged to put it in terms of prison. " A v e t e f a t t o l a p r i g i o n e ? "

" Sì sì." A fine rueful gesture. " Qualche giorno."

A few days in prison, and what for ? "P e r c h e c o s a ?"

" Magari ! " Arrigo Bellini taps his wrist, " quel orologio d'oro." This wretched wrist watch.

"*A l t r o* o r o l o g i o d ' o r o ?" the Chairman asks aghast, " D o v e ? Where ? "

No no, quello lì. This one, Thursday night's, here.

The second judge tries to elucidate the difference between custody and a previous prison sentence.

Schaffhausen: A Law Case

"Ehhh ! è prigione," says the young man and looks suddenly bored.

"S'accomodi," says the Chairman and Arrigo Bellini sits down. This time there is a discreet, green-uniformed policeman in the background.

The public prosecutor now reads the act of accusation in High German. The story of the crime has been all over town, accurately for once.

No oath is taken. There exists no form of oath in this Canton.

"È vero?" asks the Chairman.

"Eh sì," says the accused.

Nevertheless, the bench puts it all again to him, in translation, phase by phase. On Thursday, on that December afternoon, at nightfall, Signor Bellini had arrived in town? He had walked from the railway station through the lighted streets ... The shops were open, fruit and pastry stalls were blazing in the market square ... He had been directed to an inn of good repute, z'Blu Krutz, andava alla Croce Azzurra? Aveva una valigia? Yes, yes, he had a suitcase.

On the stairs of the Blue Cross Inn, scrubbing, he saw a girl. Ha visto una ragazza?

"Vedevo une signorina. Era bella."

He looked at her. She looked at him. Fu com' un colpo. He spoke, she gaped. He spoke again—in vain. She could not understand. Non ci potevamo capire. He dashed into the street, into the first well-lit *bijouterie*, a tray stood on the counter, seized a small gold bracelet watch, a pretty little watch, dashed out, ran, mind on return—put it at her feet : a gesture, a sign.

"Il orologio vale 298 franchi?"

"Il valore non ho visto."

But the woman behind the counter had had no trouble at all, two steps outside the Blue Cross and her hand was on his lapel.

Since, he had wept, raged, in turns laughed at himself.

"Allora, quel gesto——?" the Chairman says, "*ero* un gesto?"

The public prosecutor wishes to know if the young man realises that he did wrong.

The judges withdraw and the accused stays with us. The *Waibel*, not smoking himself, produces a cigarette.

When the sentence is announced it is thirty days deferred. He may go now, says the Chairman.

" Signor," the young man says with a touch of haughtiness, " you sent me to prison,"

"È una pena condizionata," says the Chairman. No more presents to young ladies—no prison. After five years it will even be wiped off the record. "Capito?"

"No, Signore."

"Trenta giorni di prigione condizionata."

" Prigione ? "

"Condizionata."

" Niente prigione," says the Waibel.

" Sì sì," says the young man.

"E una pena condizionata," says the judge.

The young Italian raises imploring eyes to the policeman to get him out of so much fussing and confusion.

III

Bâle

Happy Half-Cantons have no history. On Dr. K.'s advice I spent two weeks in a metropolis ; I went to Bâle, that large, industrialised and most prosperous town on the Swiss Rhine. Here, too, the law courts were housed in an old and friendly building ; below the windows there grew trees ; in the carpeted court-rooms, gold-framed sombre oils hung upon the walls, stags at the brook, the Judgment of Paris, Alpine sunrise. Here, too, the men on the bench had patrician faces and used the same extravagantly homely speech. Here, too, the judges could not do enough for the stranger in their court, opening minds and chambers, offering guidance, answers, questions, books. Here, too, at the hearings the same simplicity, the absence of professional aloofness, the same slow sympathy and care, the natural pace of patience, the concern with individual dignity and communal well-being, the backing of the petty rule as well as the small change of freedom. And here, too, the humdrum dailiness of the cases— mild civil disputes, infringed regulations, small crime. And in every ante-room there ruled a *Waibel*, dressed, at the High Court of Bâle, in morning-coat and white tie, wielding a large stocking-purse full of silver money, proffering comfort and advice, adding his word at times to the proceedings and generally behaving as butlers do in novels.

The absence of mumbo-jumbo, of professional side, goes further than the mere spurning of wig and gown, the tweed jacket on the Criminal Bench, the dark lounge suit in the Court of Appeal, it springs from the Swiss sense of the community of citizens, from their dislike of specialisation, and from a humanistic inheritance, a still living conviction that—outside of science at least—all branches of human activity are open to all men. Their farmer is also a locksmith and a vintner and a shipwright and in the evening mends the clocks; the artisan keeps books; the chartered accountant runs a saw mill and the county council; the woodcutter has a chair of modern history. There's things you do in winter, they say, and things you do in summer, you can't sit in a chair all year. And so the law, too, is felt to be something that can be administered by any able-minded man of good repute. There is also the fact of a long past of political equality : since 1291 every Swiss, unless a cretin, has been a natural member of the ruling class.

The people do not only vote the laws and elect the judges, there is a cordial and adult relationship between bench and public in the courts. Not that there is much public : a rare sensational trial here as elsewhere draws full courts, but there is a complete absence of that penful of people who come for a bit of warmth and a bit of life, to gape and doze, which is a fixture of the criminal courts of England, France and Germany. Here it is more the young and studious, in groups, in clubs, in classes—a dozen baker's apprentices with their master taking in a commercial case, a company of insurance clerks, a sharp-shooters' association on a semi-outing. The judge asks them who they are; they do not hesitate to put him questions. It's like this, he will say, and keep them back after a case to tell them the reason why.

"Now, how would *you* have handled this ? " A woman had been kicking up an unholy fuss about her savings account.

The youth thinks hard. " *D'Frue isch v'ruckt.* "

Yawyaw, maybe, says the judge, he could see she was a bit touched, but he had had to look at the post-office savings

book all the same. " *Der objektive Tatbestand,* young man.
We always have to look at the evidence."
The boy drinks it in. All this does not in the least impair
the dignity of the court. Perhaps the contrary.
" Now, what would have happened in England ? "
I suppose, I said, that if the case had got to court at all,
the plaintiff would have been in the dock for attempting to
break the peace in a post office.
The judge shook his head. " *S'Postscheckbüchli*—there was
something not in order with the little savings book.

Order, out of order, not in order, these are words heard
constantly from every bench. Another one is *Recht*; it serves
for Right, Just, Justice, Legal, the Law. It must serve for
Fair. The term does not exist. Anything like a sporting
notion is alien to these parts ; not right is wrong—out of
order—out of joint—out of repair. There can be no other
reaction than to put it right. Swiss justice works in terms
of clock-making, you don't give a fast fly-wheel the benefit
of the doubt or another chance, you prize up the case, look
inside and try to set it back.

And how hard they work ! Longer hours, cheerfully, than
their proverbially toiling neighbours further up the Rhine.
West-Germans, attracted into Switzerland by lower taxes
and high pay, are said to slink back after a time crushed by
overwork. The Swiss carry on. At Bâle, in grey winter
drizzle, there are cases beginning at eight-fifteen ; at Zurich
in summer the high court regularly opens at seven a.m. But in
the evening all sit in the taverns over wine, there is ski-ing,
walking, bathing in the lakes, and the country, everywhere,
is at easy uncrowded reach. One hears no talk of ulcers,
no-one is ever pressed or in a temper or a hurry, and over
every phase of living there is spread a soothing layer of deep-
bred placidity.
    The Swiss are hard-headed. They know the values and are

willing to pay the price. They chose material order, moral regularity and that very hard-earned communal good, unconditional non-aggression. There is of course no capital punishment, and has not been, in three-quarters of the Cantons, for over eighty years. There is of course no question of flogging. There is of course no anti-homosexual law. Pragmatists, paragons of enlightened self-interest and—always —humanists, they have known how to keep a man-sized world, and through the sometimes stern, sometimes pedestrian tissue of their life there runs an enduring streak of douceur de vivre.

The Swiss Judges' Rules, the safeguards against primitive or oppressive forms of criminal investigation, are explicitly codified in some of the Cantons. Here is an example.

Article 73.* Personal liberty is guaranteed. No-one may be arrested except in the circumstances and forms prescribed by the law [minutely detailed below]. The law determines compensation due in cases of unlawful arrest.

Article 76. A private house is inviolate. No public servant or employee of the police may enter a private dwelling place except in the cases and forms prescribed by the law. Personal resistance against unlawful entry is permitted.

Article 106. Means likely to induce a suspected person to give evidence, and in particular means calculated to produce a confession, such as the use of force or constraint, threats, promises, misrepresentations or leading questions, are forbidden. Infractions of this rule will be dealt with disciplinarily, and may also be subject of a subsequent criminal prosecution.

Article 115. After arrest the examining justice must

* Gesetz über das Strafverfahren des Kanton's Bern. 20. *Mai.* 1928.

immediately notify the family of the arrested man. Should the family find itself in a position of need, the local assistance office must be informed at once.

Bâle is a very rich Canton. There are no poor. Private and public money is spent freely. Taxes are just and not too high. The young are well brought up. God is feared and the family is loved. Crimes against property are committed mainly by psychopaths and foreign workers. Nevertheless the summary courts do not stand idle. The Swiss appear to have a passion, almost equal to the Germans', for dragging their private rows before the courts. Charges of slander, vilification, back-biting and evil-speaking are for ever poured —not reticently—into the patient judge's ear by waitresses, landlords, van drivers, neighbours and meddling passers-by.

"*Brülle muschtz net,*" the Waibel cautions a furious couple who have come to howl a duet about an intolerable smell of cigar in their flat.

"He smokes them through our key-hole."

"Would you mind saying that again?" says the judge.

The defendant, a reasonable-looking man, who lives in the flat across the landing, denies this with a shrug, His wife confirms him.

The couple persists—great cloud of foul smoke puffed into their home out of sheer malice. The *Dreckspeck.*

The judge says, "Really now . . ."

The defendant says that he may well sometimes have smoked on the common staircase.

The judge says there is no law against it. "What brand do you smoke?"

"Toscani."

"*Not* Toscani," says the judge. "*Oh. Oh. Toscani.* My good man. . . . Of course they go through key-holes."

Next is a service daughter complaining she has been unjustly taxed with ironing holes into the table napkins. She did not iron those napkins, that particular lot went to the laundry. She swears it did, she saw the bundle going off.

Unlike Schaffhausen, the courts of Bâle may administer an oath. They use it with economy. The form of words goes like a Schumann Lied, " Niemand zu lieb, niemand zu leid." There is also a form of hand oath.

" Can you give me a *Handgelübdte* ? " the judge said, " then give me your hand on it." The girl stepped up and they shook hands.

Then a taxi driver claimed compensation for dismissal without notice. The company manager gave evidence that the man was unpunctual, lazy and rude.

The judge said, yaw shoah, but it wasn't enough for a straight dismissal.

There was more to come, said the manager. Herr Aleck would not wear Christian clothes to work, he wouldn't wear his driver's uniform, he objected to the trousers. He had them altered.

Perhaps they didn't fit, said the judge.

Nanei, it wasn't the fit, it was the cut. Herr Aleck said they were too wide. He had them altered—altered, well, into something more à la cowboy.

A bearded professor had been running across the road heading for his tram, he bumped into a schoolgirl on a bicycle, the girl fell, the professor made for the tram ; indignant passengers pulled him off and here he is hurled before the bench. The parents are here, too, suing for a pair of stockings and the doctor's bill. *Mit Zins*. Interest.

Next one horrid woman alleged that when she came home one night from the cinematograph another horrid woman had been hanging out of an upper window, spying on her. The other woman said it was well after midnight and she'd been leaning out for a breath of air.

Bâle

The impertinence, said the first. Cinematograph, my eye, said the second.

Then there came a whole group who complained of a messenger boy who would whistle at them when they went out to hang their washing in the yard. The boy said it was his luncheon hour, and by no means at all of them.

The judge said, " That amounts to an admission, you know." The boy laughed.

There was worse to come.

A black-suited man with the countenance of Mr. Murdstone stood up and handed a letter to the court. It was an anonymous letter, addressed to himself. It was read out. It was not a pleasant letter.

" Stop trying to turn your office into a concentration camp. Everyone knows you are a tyrant and a sadist, but they don't respect you. Your employees kotow to you but they laugh at you behind your back. We could unfold a pretty tale to your hard-used wife. Your connection with a girl of nineteen is common knowledge. You ought to be ashamed of yourself!!"

Mr. Murdstone now tendered a second letter. It was from his wife and addressed to the court. Her husband, she wrote, had sent police to ask her questions. She preferred to admit that she herself was the author of the anonymous letter. She begged to be excused attendance. " To appear before you opposite my husband is more than I can face." Her allegations about the girl of nineteen, she added, were the truth.

This was a private prosecution, brought by Mr. Murdstone. The judge asked him if he wished to go on with it.

He bowed gravely. Yes.

Presently an elderly stick of a man appeared and stated that he was a bank clerk by occupation ; every evening for two years he had gone to the Gasthaus Swan and helped the owner, the widow Swan, to make up her daily accounts, he had never been paid a franc and he now wished to claim his fee.

The widow Swan, round and elderly, stepped forward to say she had understood that he was helping her with the books and correspondance because she was a woman alone and none too good at figures. They had taken supper together evening after evening in the back-room. A *good* supper.

The judge said, " Was there any kind of agreement, was it a business arrangement ? "

" No, more of a love arrangement."

In that case, said the judge, the court was not competent.

The Waibel bowed them out. " That," he said in ringing tones, " is what makes the world go round."

IV

Une Prisonnière

Swiss litigation is not all geranium pots, postal savings and canary feed. The Swiss are discreet bankers to half the world. Foreign cash deposits, foreign paper holdings, foreign companies that are companies by a name plate and an *homme de paille*, the dictator's nest-egg and the second Maharanee's diamonds. At Zurich, at Geneva, the walls of the sanctuaries are solid, but sometimes an echo of transactions will reach the courts. I saw the co-heiress to one of the greatest contemporary fortunes sued for a lawyer's bill running to some thousands of pounds in an action that was only a side-shoot of a concurrent one in the Bâle courts for the recovery of a Million Swiss francs worth of bonds, an action which in its turn was but a tributary to the main Jarndyce *v.* Jarndyce that had been crawling its hydra course through the French courts for the last fourteen years and with no end in view.

The atmosphere of the case was sheer literature and very depressing. Mademoiselle Z., the heroine-victim, sat with her supporters. No longer young, thin-lipped, flat-chested, shabby, vivacious and defiant—*la province française entière à son but attachée*. The issue, here, was straightforward. Mlle. Z. had been unable to pay the lawyer she had retained for the Swiss branch of her lawsuit, and the lawyer, a local man, reluctant but by now himself at the end of his tether, was suing for his outlays and his fee (a course permitted to lawyers on the Continent). He did not appear and was represented by a confrère. Mlle. Z., unwilling or unable to plead her own cause, had managed to secure the services of yet another lawyer. He was youngish and in his way tried to do his best for her. There was no question of disputing his colleague's claim ; the claim was just, the expenses out of his own pocket were huge, the claim was overdue—only at this stage of her affairs Mlle. Z. was totally unable to meet it. Mlle. Z. was living in a furnished room at Lausanne, earning her living by working in daytime at an office ; at night she typed her own pleadings. She disposed of no other means, had no resources, and if judgment in the present case went against her, she would find herself unable to go on at law—it would be the end for her, final ruin, the triumph of her enemies, her family. Whereas if payment of this mounting tide of costs might be once more deferred, this harassed lady would be able to pursue and one day meet all her liabilities out of her due and legal share of her father's immense fortune.

" Mademoiselle Z. is a victim of High Capitalism, a victim of the dynastic mentality of her family," the young lawyer declaimed bravely. The five judges sat, sad and stolid.

Here was the true story. Some fifteen years ago old Monsieur Z., head of the Z. Empire had died, leaving four children, three sons, engaged in directing the various branches of the Z. works, and one daughter. Mlle. Z. claimed her legal share in her father's estate. Her brothers refused outright. No woman in their family had ever dreamt of moving off with an independent share of the Z. capital, except for their portion as a bride ; Mlle. Z., unmarried, need only stay at home in comfort. Mlle. Z. had not wished to stay at home. She was, the lawyer said, an independent spirit ; she had at one time been something of a patron of the arts, she was, he said, herself a bit of an artist. In fine she had not wished to live in her brothers' home, playing the maiden aunt. . . . Here he somewhat floundered. The Swiss, who have no more stomach for the emancipation of their women than French dynastic industrialists, looked non-committal.

Une Prisonnière

The brothers persisted in their refusal to share out the inheritance. They proposed she either stay, or take five million French francs in cash—at the time some five thousand pounds—and sign a deed of renunciation. She went to law. The brothers countered with obstruction, backed by the vast means at their disposal. Mlle. Z. was unable to pay her lawyers; her brothers had a law firm of their own. Mlle. Z., late in life, had to start to earn her daily bread ; her brothers, taking advantage of the fact that their late father's ramified possessions were left—it had been towards the end of the German Occupation—in a state of perhaps not involuntary confusion, were able to swell and multiply the law suits and drag out the years. Several times already the French courts of lower instance had found for Mlle. Z., each time there had been an appeal and a new issue raised as well. Even this lawyer's bill, the subject of the present litigation, had solely been incurred in consequence of a decision of a French court that before proceeding to any partition there must be furnished a complete inventory of the Z. estate. Now, old Monsieur Z. had floated a Swiss company under a cover name in the 1940's, the holdings of which it was well-nigh impossible to trace. The brothers Z. sat back, not lifting a finger. Their sister spent several years in the Swiss courts and incurred a small fortune's worth of debts in the process. This, then, was the background of a tale of fourteen years of penury and frustration, fourteen years of a struggle against phantoms. " I have spoken."

As the lawyer sat down, one of the supporters wanted him to start again and bring in what the maid had been told to do at Mlle. Z.'s mother's death-bed. Mlle. Z. signalled him to desist.

There was no answer. One did not hear—in this court— the other side. Plaintiff's counsel responded with an exercise in shuffling—it was obvious that the creditor lawyer wanted at least a legal handle to his money ; he also did not seem to wish to harm his former client and her future chances—there

217

was a hint here and there of intransigeance on her part, of antagonising attitudes, but as an argument it drifted like a slit bed of feathers. " I have spoken."

The judges reserved judgment. One of them later on said to me, " That's an old old story—a true labyrinth—*on n'en sortira jamais.* But believe me, there is something not in order in that family."

I went to meet Mlle. Z., who believed she had found a champion, at the hotel by the railway station. It was evening ; I found her in the café installed with her chief supporter. He was nearly an old man, bearded, wearing a thick, slightly spotty, pepper-and-salt suit, and not quite of her own class. There were glasses of tea and lemon, full and empty, on the table, over-flowing ashtrays, and the rest of the space was covered with bundles of legal and financial papers. She introduced him as her *homme d'affaires* and *fidèle ami.* He addressed her as Mademoiselle ; she called him Docteur. In court, Mlle. Z. and her history had appeared to have been descended from that rich and narrow line that runs from Balzac to M. François Mauriac ; in this hotel, this café, at this table with this protector and companion, a shift became visible into a less French world, here she might have been, or almost, the well-bred girl from Saint Petersburg, her edges coarsened by poverty and contact with bohemia, plotting high-mindedly in this very country with Vladimir Stefanovich, eternal student, idealist, humble admirer, adviser, hanger-on.

" He can tell you," she said.

" Ah, if you read this—— If you read that—— And that." He shoved one more wad into my hands. They were typed on flimsy paper with weak ribbons. " Here is the judgment of Grenoble."

" *C'est trop long,*" Mlle. Z. said with a touch of dryness.

They had trunkfuls of them in her room, they said. A thousand files. Here was only some stuff they wanted to go through on this trip. Presently they were expecting a man with

Une Prisonnière

some news of the missing bonds ; later in the evening they hoped to have a conference with the new lawyer. . . .

"*Quelle affaire!*" And I, she said, must tell the world. "What is the name of your newspaper?"

I told her the disappointing truth, I was a free-lance, a writer.

"But you can sometimes get something into a review?"

I said it was a possibility.

"*Alors?*"

He put a piece of string around another bundle and resolutely laid it in front of me. "Above all you mustn't believe half they tell you. There's no justice to be found in the Swiss courts," he said with a glint. "Not in financial litigation, not in cases like this one. We *know.*"

Mlle. Z. sighed.

What about France?

"They can't do anything against my brothers. Oh, in the lower courts, perhaps ; the lower courts are all right, *ce sont des braves gens.*" She added, "Do you have an idea how rich we are?" She still used We, like royalty in exile. "You do know what we make?"

I said it would be hard to have remained unaware of their fast and gleaming product.

"Oh, that," she said, "that was something my father got interested in as a young man." The real money, the big money—and when she said *l'argent*, it was again as Balzac might have heard it—that came from a little thing, no bigger than a hairpin, in universal use, found at every iron-monger's.

"*Why* do you think Mademoiselle's lawyer brought this suit against her?" he said.

I agreed that it was difficult to see where the money was to come from, even if he got his judgment.

"Oh, he'll get his judgment. He'll get his judgment. [Hollow laugh] Let me tell you what's behind it—they want to force Mademoiselle to her knees."

"Her own lawyer?"

He whispered. " He's been bought."

I said to her, " How can you explain it ? "

" My brothers can't accept a woman who wants her rights. I asked them for accounts, it was an outrage ; they've never forgiven me."

" Do you ever see them ? "

" *Au tribunal.*"

I said : *must* this go on ? Could there be not a compromise —not of course the five million francs—something to make life liveable again, something to take and go away in peace.

She said, " You don't know my family. *Et puis ils sont entêtés mes frères . . .*" then with a sudden wry smile, " We all are. Mules."

Soon there was nothing but to go. If you can, I tried to say, don't let it swamp you, don't let it swamp the whole of life.

" Oh, you know, *c'est une façon de vivre.* I've got used to it, *Cela m'occupe.* It's a better life than I should have had at home. *Avec mes belles-sœurs . . . Et puis au fond,*" she raised her thin shoulders, " *Je m'amuse.*"

She wrote her address in my diary. I have it now. If I ever pass through Lausanne I may dare go and ask how the law suits are getting on. Well, I hope.

At the door I had to turn round to unhook my coat, Mlle. Z. and her protector were already plunged back in their law files, back in their chosen way of life.

PART FOUR

FRANCE

I

Paris—La Cour d'Assises

Scarlet on the tribune, at the high end of the ornate hall, the togaed judges loom, robed like inquisitors, enthroned like kings of cards.

Above them gilt and mouldings, an emphatic ceiling; below, empty, a space of floor; beyond, wave after wave of advocates in billowing black, and beyond, at the far end, behind a grille, on their feet: the people, *la foule parisienne*, pressed by guards. Police everywhere; police the length and breadth, in parade dress, red kepi and white belt, in all the aisles, at every side-door.

We are a far cry here from those Alpine commons where for seven hundred years the magistrate was named by his peers, the yeomen, by a showing of raised hands; we are back among the trappings of authority, the pomp and ceremony and the remoteness of justice. Yet it is not the atmosphere of Assizes in England. The tradition is not the same.

When the fanfares sound and his Lordship in procession passes through the streets, an Englishman's response may be some comfortable image of Magna Carta, Habeas Corpus and the Common Law; French associations with the Cour d'Assises, the *Palais*, or even simply justice, might be the Police State of the Ancien Régime, the Tribunal of the Revolution, the Napoleonic Code, the Commune, the Police State of Napoleon III and the present prerogatives of the Police.

France

A lateral door leading straight into a three-tiered stall now opened, there was a jingling noise and the accused stepped through the low opening, one man after another, twelve of them, each handcuffed, each chained by a short link to a policeman. Before they sat down, each man turned sideways in the confined space and faced his guard, holding out his pair of hands. Each guard produced and tinkered with a tiny key, unlocked cuffs and chain, hung them in his belt. This took several minutes, while the court sat suspended ; then the box was filled, the tiers complete, a man next to a policeman next to a man next to a policeman, like three rows of piano keys. All the twelve accused were Arabs, Algerians.

The jury, a fused jury as in Germany, were called and took their seats on the tribune with the judges and the representative of the prosecution, the Avocat général. There were nine of them, eight men and one woman.

Below the bench stood a glass case exhibiting a heap of labelled fire-arms, a mixed collection ranging from two or three small automatics and some army colts to a long-handled museum pistol.

The trial opened with the reading of the *acte d'accusation*. This was an extremely involved, one might say confusing document as it charged twelve separate people with having respectively committed or taken part singly, severally or jointly, on one or two or more or all of six separate crimes. Some of the men were charged with murder, some with two or three murders, some with conspiracy and some with complicity to murder.

The first of these crimes took place in the town of Metz in May 1956. It was an armed attack upon a café kept by an Algerian. The owner was killed, another Algerian wounded, some French customers slightly wounded, and the café smashed. A second similar attack on another small Algerian café in the same district was carried out five days later, on May 10th. The attacks continued through May and June and ceased after the sixth one in July. In all there were about half a dozen people killed and a greater number hurt, among them a town night-watchman in the execution of his duty. The killers in each instance had worn thick stockings drawn over their faces. No-one had been caught in the act, no-one had been arrested at the time.

It should be noted that all these fact were gleaned piecemeal —by jury, press and public—in the course of the trial from depositions, examinations, witnesses and even closing speeches. The French system, like the German, Austrian and Swiss, does not provide for a presentation of the case.

The alleged motive of the crimes was political. The twelve accused—arrested on various dates in the course of the police inquiry—had been in custody, *prison préventive*, between three and three and a half years. The present trial took place in December 1959. It was held in Paris because it was believed that these men could not be tried at Metz, without provoking incidents. In fact incidents were feared in Paris also, and a strict eye was kept on admissions.

"Ghabi Mohamède Assenen——!"

The first major phase of a trial at French Assizes consists of the oral examination of the accused. It is carried out, exclusively, by the presiding judge, the Président des Assises.

The man who sat in the right-hand corner of the lowest tier of the box stood up and delivered in Arabic what sounded like a virile harangue.

He was a slightly-built man, though hard, with a sallow, clean-shaven, expressionless face and very dark hair. He might have been thirty or fifty. In an evening street, at a casual glance, one could have taken him for a native of Lisbon, or Brazil. It was only once one knew him to be Arab that one could not see him as anything else : an Arab who had lived in cities a long time.

An interpreter took the floor. He looked like a Gallicized Hindu, wizened, hairless and pot-bellied, and every inch a *fonctionnaire*. He translated into direct speech.

"I shall not talk. You have insulted our language. You forbade us the use of our language. I shall be silent."

Tell him, said the Président, that he has the right to answer the charges made against him; in his own language if he so desires. The Président's voice was clipped and cold.

The interpreter turned to the box, and from this little man, also, the words sounded like the cry of the muezzin. Then came another bolt from the accused.

Interpreter: "On our way to the court the guards in the van forbade us to speak to each other in our language."

Président: "Une excellente mesure de la part de vos gardiens, dont je les félicite."

The accused man sat down, folded his arms and fixed the Président with a slight smile. One gained the impression that he understood, and probably spoke, French perfectly.

"Ali Rachime——!"

A man in a belted mackintosh, in his forties perhaps, a pasty face, a little moustache, small eyes, low-growing hair—not a pleasant face. He half rises, chants a line, slumps back.

Interpreter: "I do not seek to understand. I do not wish to answer."

Président: "*Bon.*"

"Abdel Hafir Mohamède——!"

Splendid shoulders straining the store-bought jacket, a warrior's stance, glowing skin, long black moustaches, a pointed beard, a furrowed forehead and huge vacant eyes. He uncoiled his height, spat his word, sat back and looked at nothing.

Interpreter: "I stand ready to be judged. I stand ready to die.

Président: "*Parfait.*"

"Ali Saïd——!"

Interpreter: "I shall not speak. I accept in advance the decision of the judge."

Paris: La Cour d'Assises

And so on right to the last man in the last seat on the highest tier.

The twelve counsel for the defence had not stirred.

The Président said, " So this is to be their attitude—a system of silence. The gentlemen of the jury will appreciate it."

No answers—no questions. Instead, the Président had to resort to reading the accused men's depositions, one after the other, *extracts* from the depositions, out of the high pile of dossiers in front of him. Out came a tissue of statements and counter statements, made to the police, made to the Juge d'instruction, containing admissions, confessions, retractions, inculpating now one man, now another, shifting, qualifying, passing on the focal points of guilt. Some of the men admitted membership of the F.L.N., the Algerian terrorist organisation, others professed their total ignorance ; some men named the two or three whom they believed to be the leaders of the local cell, the men so designated persisted in denial ; some confessed to having acted from conviction, others under orders, still others repeated—after months of interrogation—that they had been pressed into participation under threats.

The victims of the attacks were Algerians who had refused or ceased to pay the contributions levied by the F.L.N. They were residents of France, people in a small way, many of them vaguely relapsed Mohammedans who had already put themselves beyond the pale by their adopted western ways. The attacks were supposed to serve as warnings as well as liquidations. They followed a certain routine. A couple of men would burst into a café at a crowded hour and begin to overturn the tables, smash looking-glasses, bottles, lights ; in the uproar another man would step on quietly, fire a few wild shots then make for the man behind the bar and sometimes for his family as well.

" ' On the night before the attack on Ali Mouchi, I met a man whose name I believe to be Achmède in the public

227

convenience of the rue de la Boucherie. I received from him a Mauser pistol .32. The meeting had been arranged by the man Rachime.'

" We now come to the affaire of the couple Elluli.

" ' On June 11th I received the visit of a man who was unknown to me. I have since identified him with the accused Saïd——'

" L'affaire Miramil—— L'affaire Nouachi—— L'affaire Fétallah—— "

As it reeled on, there emerged a pattern of division into leaders, killers, wreckers. The identities of the wreckers at least were clear. There were five of them, *les casseurs de café* the Président called them ; they were the youngest among the accused and they had all confessed. They were charged with being accessories ; they maintained they were cat's-paws, dragged from their lodgings, picked up in the street, by unknown compatriots, razor or gun in hand, persuaded to come along. All five to the end had denied any connection with the F.L.N.

Abdel Hafir, the one who looked like a tribesman without his spear, had admitted a number of the killings : he had been ordered to liquidate so-and-so, finish off such-and-such. Ali Rachime, the man in the mackintosh, had been connected with the giving or transmitting of some of the orders, with the passing of fire-arms and with several of the killings. Neither the police nor the Juge d'instruction had been able to establish the slightest physical connection between the attacks and Ghabi M. Assenen, the first of the accused. He was believed to have been the moving power behind the scenes and the chief of the *casbah*, the regional committee of the F.L.N. This he had denied throughout. As he sat there with his thin smile, neither alert nor wholly relaxed, one became impressed by the sense of some ghastly concentric games of cat and mouse. *He* knew what he knew and that *they* knew that he knew more than they knew, and that they could not prove it. *They* knew that he knew what he knew they could not get at, but *they* knew and *he* knew that they would be able to act as if they could, or nearly.

In France, hearings in the high courts begin early in the afternoon and go on well into the night. The reading of those depositions droned on hour after hour, punctuated only at the end of each man's file by his brief word of refusal to hear the translation. The jury sat, the way juries do ; the Président read, turned pages, selected, read on. Below, advocates came and went, leaned over a brother, shook a hand without a glance, whispered three words, tip-toed away, thick satchel under arm—lawyers without wigs, they looked like so many Frenchmen from every walk of life.

The prosecutor's pulpit at the Assises overhangs the press stall, and there within arm's reach was the still torso of the Avocat général the statue of a man, sharp-faced, ascetic, who wore the toga well. The press stall was not crowded, France has had a surfeit of such things ; an observer, from some ministry, sat tracing arabesques upon the fly-leaf of his note-book. Opposite, face to face, the fixed sight, inescapable, of those twelve by twelve—the Algerian faces and, wedged pink or white or blue-chinned between the képi and the collar of the uniform, the faces of their guards, the *flics*. The record of the sordid tangle went on and on in the same dust terms, one listened, one looked, one listened : there appeared no connection, no resolvent, no light, and it is hard to convey the monotony, the hopelessness, the sense of deadlock, of that afternoon.

Once there was a short interval, a *suspension d'audience* ; the bench retired, the men stood up, turned, held out their joined hands. Again there was the clanking, the jangling, the silver clicks, the delays ; then they filed out. Ten minutes later, the court resumed : the same process.

The trial lasted four days. The second was the day of *témoins et experts*, witnesses and experts. Again the hearing began at one p.m. These hours are kept to outmanoeuvre the effects of luncheon, no jury of true Frenchmen can be trusted to keep their eyes open after that meal (luncheon at home at an unduly early hour is not considered the same). The custom has been going on for a good hundred years, and today members of the Paris Bar still eat at half past eleven. The chief expert was a ballistics man. As there were thirteen disowned fire-arms in the case, some retrieved in sewers, some found in a station cab in the Saar, it had been quite a job to get them all to match with the right shot, casualty and cartridge shell. Even so, according to the defence, it was not a perfect fit. One of the defence counsel had prepared a list of searching questions.

During a French trial, counsel for the defence is not really heard until his own closing speech. If he wants to put a question to a witness he can only do so with the permission and through the intermedium of the president of the court.

" Monsieur le Président, a simple question——"

" Monsieur le Président, *one* brief question——"

" Monsieur le Président—I do not think it would be wasting the court's time—if I might——"

" Monsieur le Président, with respect, it *is* material——"

The first witness for the prosecution was the police official from Metz who had been in charge of the inquiry.

The Président said, " Monsieur le Commissaire Principale ! Do take your coat off if you wish."

The Commissaire did so, hung it over a stall and went to take his place by the token bar in the middle of the floor.

English high police officers generally look tall and trim, French ones run more to the figures and faces of Russian cabinet ministers.

The police evidence consisted of the reading of another long and perhaps somewhat opaque dossier, some shots in the dark from the defence, courageously delivered and none too well received, and some honeyed words from the Président at the end.

Paris: La Cour d'Assises

A lot of it would have been inadmissible in England. " As far as I was told—in my opinion—he said to him he had heard——"

There were hints of irregularities, pressure. . . . Was it not true—this from the defence—that in the case of Mahoum the police had returned to question him some weeks after the Juge d'instruction had been seized with the case? Once the word torture fell, distinctly.

The Commissaire, steered by questions from the bench, stressed the length and complexity of the inquiry and affirmed his view that the attitude of all the agents of the police had been correct. He left the floor having received formal congratulations on his conduct of the affair.

There were only a handful of civilian witnesses in the entire case. Four of them were Algerians, and a lamentable lot : poor, timid, inarticulate, and very likely frightened to death as well.

The first was one of the café owners. He had been shot at and wounded. He spoke no French.

" *Que savez vous sur cette affaire* ? " The Président, through the interpreter, asked him to describe the attack.

" When the shooting began I went under the bar. A man leaned over it and shot."

" Did you recognise him ? "

" No."

" Can you describe him in any way ? "

" No."

" You must have seen whether he was tall or short ? "

" No."

" Did you notice what he wore ? "

" No."

" Was he at all like anyone you see here ? Please look."

[Hardly looking] " No."

" When you came out of hospital, you sold the café and you and your wife decided to leave Metz. Is that so ? "

" Yes."

" Where did you move to ? "

" Lyon."

" Did you and your wife start another café there ? "

" Yes."

" Was it the subject of another armed attack ? "

" Yes." (Another trial, in another town.)

" You are quite certain you can give us no indication as to your aggressors ? "

" Yes."

The next witness was that man's son. He was frail and small and one would have taken him for about fourteen. His age was nineteen. He spoke some French. " *Que savez vous sur cette affaire* ? " He had been present during the attack. He had seen everything and recognised nobody.

The third man was an Algerian resident of Metz and a customer of the café. He said No to every question.

The fourth was also an Algerian and a customer and he was the only witness in the case, except the night-watchman, who identified one of the accused.

" You told us he wore a thick stocking over his face ? "

" Yes."

" You recognized him nevertheless ? "

" Yes."

" Who was it ? "

" Abdel Hafir."

" Is he here ? "

" Yes."

" Will you point him out to the lady and gentlemen of the jury."

There was a curious long moment when the witness turned to the stall, faced them, and raised a hand to point. Neither he nor any of the men wore any expression at all.

Afterwards that witness was permitted to leave court.

The last of the witnesses was a poor devil of a Frenchman, burly and grinning, who had been sitting with his more affluent counsel on chairs directly below the tribune. He was the third party in the case, that special feature of French and other Continental criminal proceedings, *la partie civile*. He was the night-watchman who had been shot up at Metz.

We had all stood next to him and his tall *maître* during intermissions—advocates and press used the same entrance behind the tribune, hung about in the same little anteroom—shaken hands, smoked, expressed sympathy and concern; and everybody had rather taken to that friendly, ursine man who told his story freely, if deprecatively. Just his luck: there he was on his bicycle in the rue de la Boucherie, about to go on duty, when there was all this noise and shots and he saw this Arab chap running out of the Café de l'Espérance with a gun in his hand, well—what could he do? Go after him . . . " Croyez-moi, j'en avais pas envie. J'avais mon uniforme, qu'est-ce que j'aurais pris ! Et puis il fallait bien . . ."

Round the corner on the Boulevard, not a soul—and it was pitch—he caught up with him, jumped off and on his back, the chap whipped round, " I tried to get a grip on his arms, he still had the gun, I could feel it, alors là, j'avais peur! Ne me descends pas, je dis, j'ai trois gosses . . . Eh bien, il m'a eu, dans le ventre."

Hospital; convalescent home; half-pay. Maintenant ça va—à peu près. No, not the big one, Saïd, the little dark chap, on the left in the second row ; they got him the month after. —Oh, it's been like that all the time since the war in Algiers . . . just his luck to get mixed up in their affairs.

He'd been told to go *partie civile*. Why not——? Compensation? Fat chance! C'est un pauv' type aussi, il était chez Renault, 25,000 balles par mois. Pas vrai, Maitre ?

The lawyer said, " Une belle partie civile joue plutôt sur les jurés."

On the third day came the *réquisitoire*, the big address by the prosecution. " La parole est à Monsieur l'Avocat général." After the dossiers, after the interpreter's cries, coherent speech; easy delivery, some elegance, the tone of moderation.

France

In cases founded so very largely on cross-confessions and circumstantial evidence of fire-arms, the quality and circumstances of the police investigation are of the greatest relevance. The Avocat général, no-one's fool, opened by taking that bull by the horns. There had been suggestions, he said, allegations—— And there he unfolded an elaborate and perhaps rather dialectical refutation of the idea of evidence unfairly or oppressively obtained. "There may have been some irregularities—[wordly smile] c'est peut-être une exigence professionnelle—— But the police does not spend their time manufacturing confessions, la police ne fabrique pas les aveux—la police cherche ! "

Now an accolade to the good night-watchman, "Un hommage—pas un hommage du bout des lèvres [vibrating voice held low] mais un hommage du fond du cœur." And then the big guns, the accused men's refusal to speak. Why, members of the jury, why ? Why this grave decision, this fateful attitude upon so puerile, so transparent a pretext ? Members of the jury—why this silence ?

Now an attempt to understand, to reach a truth. "Who are these men——? What can we know of these men——? Is any contact possible between us ? We try to understand their code, the rigours of a religion designed for other centuries than ours . . . We respect their austerities . . . They killed. Why ? They shot down people who were guilty of what ? Ils buvaient du vin et ils jouaient à la belote. Of drinking wine, of playing cards . . . people who did not wish to live like them. People who did not wish to think like them. *People who did not wish to plot with them.*

" Pour eux la distinction entre le bien et le mal est fragile. . . .

" These crimes may well have had their origins in events outside these walls . . . But, members of the jury, we are not here to decide on political first causes, we are here to judge these men for crimes committed against French common law, ici par conséquent c'est le code pénal français qui a la parole. . . ."

Paris: La Cour d'Assises

An able man, doing what he must; a man of principle doing what within his society, his place, his habits of feeling, is right. After a certain point, a man can only act as he is; his lines are laid. And so are the lines of the men opposite. Do they know it? The Avocat général's question, What can we know of these men? is at least the cry of the thinking reed across the chasm between man and man.

And last to prosecution brass-tacks. Responsibility: Ghabi Assenen, Ali Rachime, Ali Saïd and company, entirely responsible, in medical estimation, for their actions. Abdel Hafir and two of the wreckers, relative attenuation. Ghabi Assenen: no direct connection established between him and the attacks. As for that, the prosecution was not asking for anybody's head, " Je ne veux pas leur tête. What I am asking you for, members of the jury, is—for some of them—a life sentence."

The same evening, the first speeches for the defence. There are more than three thousand lawyers today at the Paris Bar. The corridors of the Palais at two p.m. are like platforms at the rush hour. Life for the many is hard. Counsel at this trial, *avocats d'office* paid from public funds, are not the stars, the *ténors du barreau*, whose every oratorical subjunctive is analysed by the public and the press. Anyone may sport a shabby gown; shoes are a give-away. Some are markedly young, one or two are sadly old; one is a woman, which is however far less of a disqualifying factor here. Many look anxious and dejected. French barristers, with no solicitors to intercept the current, stand in a more close relationship to their clients. Like energy, an element of emotion must enter into any successful representation, and while an English barrister would be more likely to feel in terms of the case, a French one feels for his man. There certainly is every sign of a bond —for the time being—between French counsel and *mon bonhomme, mon type*. There is also this, a lawyer practising at the criminal bar in France never appears for anything except the defence. Whatever the merits of a case, he must interpret it from one angle ; his job is to defend and he can no more help becoming defence-minded than the civil servant above him on the tribune, whose job is to prosecute, can help becoming the opposite.

Such specialisation also fosters a relationship between bar and bench very unlike what it is in England. The fact that we have neither a separation between, nor a hierarchy of bench and bar, that all English judges have been barristers, and that some successful barristers become judges and others choose to remain successful barristers, is one of (many) blessings of the English system.

The five counsel for the wreckers had arranged to be the first to speak. They informed the bench they would be very short. And in fact none of them spoke for longer than six minutes and their argument dove-tailed. The first made an energetic appeal for mercy and common sense. These young men, he said, maintained they had been forced into what they did ; even the prosecution did not assert more than that they had been led—led astray. Had these five young men been tried separately from their elders, they would have stood their trial years ago before another court, and their sentence there might well have been one year—they were first offenders—, perhaps even one year deferred. As it was, they had by now spent over three years in prison. He must ask the court to consider these young men's sentences as served so that at least to-morrow they might be released from their long confinement.

Each counsel added a word about his man. There had been none of the Swiss probing into moral status, or of the judicial interest in personality exercised in Germany, the accused throughout the days had been a face, a name, six dates. Such character or past, such good as could be said, was left to be unearthed by the defence, dismal little sketches of deprived existences, lonely domestic virtues and brutish fortitude.

Paris: La Cour d'Assises

Suffered from TB as a boy— Six years in France— employed as a dishwasher—shared a room with three other men— sent half his pay regularly to his mother in Algiers. Worked as a car-washer— supported his brother crippled in a work accident— tendency to TB— psychiatrist gave mental age as eleven— suffers badly from confinement. . . .

During the defence speeches, the bench continued to read and mark their dossiers, just as the nonchalant judge had done in the small town in Austria.

First counsel to speak for one of the killers was an Algerian and an unfortunate choice, as he was outstandingly inept. He opened with Montaigne, quoted from the wrong man's deposition, went on to say that the gentleman who had rented sleeping space to his client had described him as " calm, loquacious and not addicted to spirits ", then lost himself in sheer *Bouvard et Pécuchet*, " Madame, Messieurs, cela se précise, cet homme, dans ce box, a un fils et une fille." He wound up with Montesquieu and he spoke for fifty-eight minutes.

Others followed. Number seven, number eight, number nine. Always the taking of the floor, the formal opening :
" *Messieurs de la Cour, Messieurs les jurés*——"

A sequence of facts, a line of argument, " What is there, gentlemen, to link this man before you with these crimes——? Conjecture, gentlemen, conjecture, pure and simple. You will say, there is a confession. . . . *Certes, mais Messieurs . . .*"
A quotation from the classics, Pascal on compassion, Horace, Montesquieu ; a brave plea for acquittal ; Montesquieu once more ; a softening of voice—one can hear them listening —a great spurt at the end ; words ; words. Gallant efforts.

Another suspension. Once more the men gathered, taken away, packed into their van, driven to the jail through the grey cold night. The next day, another day. The last of the speeches. Guards doubled at all the entrances ; no-one gets in without a pass. Some public demonstration half expected. Ghabi Assenen's counsel was the last to speak. He spoke well.

Ghabi stood up, leaned out of the box, over his guard, in a lively movement flung out his hand—counsel turned—the two men shook hands. "*Merci Maître!*"

Last words. The interpreter back on the floor. Many now speak French. Ghabi Assenen, "Vive l'Algérie—Vive la France!" Others, "I am innocent: the true responsible is he who is not here." "I keep the silence I owe to him who is not here." "Vive la mort!" "I am not guilty, the guilty man is not here." "I have nothing to say."

Down hall, the public remains quiet.

The waiting was like any other waiting of that kind. We stood in the little room, the lawyers, our night-watchman, the young man from the ministry. The *Avocat général*, still in red, paced near us. The talk, shop. The new reforms; juries; this jury. The woman on it is the widow of a great hero of the Resistance. Will they be long——? The jury meanwhile was locked with the judges in the *chambre des délibérations* down the corridor. The English institution of the jury was taken over at the Revolution lock, stock and barrel. Like many grafted benefits it worked badly; Napoleon and a succession of later amendments modified its nature. In 1937 it became fused with the bench and its number came down from twelve to seven. Decisions—sentence as well as verdict —were by straight majority, the president of the court held the casting vote. Now, in 1959, the number of the jurors has just been put up again to nine, and the necessary majority to two thirds. No more casting vote. This means that no verdict can be arrived at without at least five of the lay votes.

Will they be long——? Well, someone says, they've got over three hundred questions. It works like this: in the council chamber members of the jury are given a list of numbered questions. 18) Do you find the Accused C guilty of the charge of murder in the second attack? Yes or No. 19) Mitigation? Yes or No. 20) Diminished responsibility? Yes or No. 21) Do you find the accused C guilty

Paris: La Cour d'Assises

of the charge of conspiracy to murder in the second attack?
Yes or No. 22) Mitigation? 23) Do you find him guilty
of conspiracy against the public safety in connection with the
second attack? Yes or No. Yes or No.

The lawyers say it's all a matter of luck. The same jury sits
with the same judges for a whole sessions, and the best you
can hope is for your case to come on second. The first case
is hopeless, the jury'll do exactly as the judges tell them,
alors qu'est-ce qu'on prend! peng—Condamnation à Mort.
By the second case they have a change of heart, " nous avons
été trop durs, must show independence "—Acquitted. By
the third they feel they've gone a bit too far, a compromise——
ten years. By the fourth, full reaction, after all the professionals
know best—Les Travaux Forcés. After that, one cannot tell
the way they'll go, it's anybody's guess. The present case is
a first.

Everybody is speaking against the system with that blend
of disillusionment, passion and defeatism that has marked so
much of French political life. The French seldom sound
hopeful on matters of public interest. Perhaps they know
best. The delays, the procedure, the rigidities, the *police*. . . .
But any qualities of the Anglo-Saxon system are overshadowed
for them by their views on our executions. Too quick, too
public. It really makes those tough and cynical men shiver.
They do not think it possible for the circumstances of a crime
to be evaluated within a matter of mere months; in France
people at least languish long enough in prison for a judicial
error to be avoided often before their trial; and they consider
it inhuman to let a condemned man, and the public,
know beforehand of the date of his execution. In France
he is not told and does not know until one morning
early the procureur and the governor come into his cell and
it will be a matter of minutes.

There is something inherently depressing about a court
at night. Vitality is low, the lighting lugubrious or too bright,

the division from any familiar life too great, one longs to be out of it, to be free, to be gone.

When the court came on, the Président resumed with " L'audience est reprise, veuillez vous asseoir." Then he read. He read for a long time. " The answer of the Court to question number one is Yes. The answer of the Court to question number two is No. The answer of the Court to question number three— to question number four— number five——" There were in all three hundred and thirty eight questions.

When the answers had been read, and only then, the accused were called up one by one.

The first of the wreckers : Five years' imprisonment ; sentence to begin with this date.

Second of the wreckers : Five years' imprisonment ; sentence to begin with this date.

Third, fourth fifth wrecker : Idem ; idem ; idem.

The first of the killers : Twenty years' hard labour. Second of the killers : Twenty years' hard labour. Ali Saïd : Hard labour for life—travaux forcés â perpétuité. Abdel Hafir : Travaux forcés à perpétuité. Ali Rachime : Travaux forcés à perpétuité. Ghabi Mohamède Assenen : Twenty years.

The man from the ministry finished marking his list. 20. 20. T.F.P. T.F.P. T.F.P. 20. " Oh, well," he said, " they may appeal." Then with that French reliance on indirect remedies, he added, " It isn't the last word, there'll be an amnesty some day."

II

Paris—Summary Justice

The sinews of litigation are papers. There are many con-
tenders, there can't be a nation recent or old that isn't in the
race, but for sheer stamina, antiquity and spread the barnacled
French bureaucracy may still be in for a prize. Across the
road from the Palais de Justice, in the basements of the
Tribunal de Commerce, there is an emporium devoted
exclusively to the scrutiny, handling and processing of forms,
a kind of infernal French post office where alpaca-coated clerks
and petitioners labour on blotchy paper with scratching pens.
The line of windows begins quite hopefully:

 * DEMANDS * * REQUESTS * * CERTIFICATES *

The pilgrim returning at the end of his third week may
have to take his place in the queue for * COPIES * or for
 * MODIFICATIONS * * EXTRACTS *

Further down the path lie,
 * OPPOSITIONS * * REVERSES * * RETARDS *

Some people put up with some things and not with others.
Much of life in France—the part of life that can be reached
and squeezed by pettifogging or puritanical legislation—
is easier, more humanised, more civilised, more agreeable.
An adult may drink a glass of beer in a public place at four

o'clock of a warm afternoon, there is no insuperable difficulty about being served a decent dinner at a decent place after ten p.m. ; food can be bought at leisure in the evening instead of having to be scrambled for as the doors are being bolted on the way back from work ; people make love in the parks. There is tolerance in practice, speech and print about sexual matters ; working people, in particular, are broad-minded, sensible and charitable.

On the other hand, the French put up with a degree of regimentation which the heavens be praised would still be unacceptable to us. They have had some form or other of a long, rough compulsory military service for centuries ; French people, all of them, must carry identity cards ; they cannot get a passport without first obtaining a certificate of *bonne vie et mœurs* from the local police station ; and they have always acquiesced in the wide, vague and vested powers of police. Not all of them, far from it, but the solid bulk of the their middle-classes and Establishment after Establishment. The Frenchman in good standing knows all about the clutches of the police and shrugs about them ; order and property have been so often threatened since 1789, the clutches are a necessary evil, perhaps not even that: just necessary, and at any rate they are only for the next man, the man beyond the pale. To the right kind of French, the police, like death to small children, is *pour les autres*. It is all as simply logical as that—the police treat people badly ; only bad people get into the clutches of the police ; bad people deserve what they get. And if the police do make a mistake—*cela arrive*—other Frenchmen in good standing can be counted on to rally and set things right and all will end in apologies and expressions of esteem and the final handshake with *Monsieur le Commissaire*. And what if one doesn't know anyone of substance or position, what if one has neither got *relations* nor *famille* and doesn't even know a *Député*? Well, then, one is simply not a Frenchman in good standing and back we are at the syllogism. The working people, though cynical enough about it all, are patient and resigned; prosperous as they are, they still have the fatalistic resignation of the poor before authority—*ah, c'est qu'ils sont mauvais! c'est qu'ils sont terribles!*, and a thief or murderer is generally referred to as *un malheureux*, and that is that; at least until the next revolutionary rising.

France—in spite of the Revolution, possibly in a measure because of the Revolution—has never been a " free country " in the sense that the English and the United States and the Dutch and the Scandinavians and the Swiss understand it. The surface of life has been good in the good times for a large number of people of reasonable virtue and of reasonable luck.

Everyone who goes to Paris has walked past the law-courts, the *Palais*, that eclectic construction, Third Empire from feudal tower, so massively planted on the Ile de la Cité between the Quai de l'Horloge and the Quai des Orfèvres. Having dinner in the Place Dauphine one sits below one portico'd façade, on one's way across the river from the Boulevard St-Michel one passes by the railings of the other side; one cannot even visit the Sainte Chapelle without coming out through one of the *Palais* yards. The inside is another matter.

Acres of vestibule and audience hall, mile on mile of gallery, stairways, passages—the stately chambers of the Civil Courts, la Première de la Court, la Sixième du Tribunal, near chapels dripping with renaissance carvings, ceilings alight with nymph and cloud; la Chambre des Requètes; la Cour de Cassation, the Courts of Criminal Appeal; the Robing Room of the Ordre des Avocats; la Chambre des Ordonnances; and down meaner aisles the warren of the Correction-nelles. Gilded vistas and grey-walled, thick-walled, twisting, narrowing tunnels leading up and down into attics and cellars, turrets, crevasses and dead-ends—to the Greffier's office, the offices of the Procureur, of the Juges d'instruction, of the Huissiers, to the quarters of the Presse Judiciaire, to the Appellate Court of the Conseil de Prud'Hommes, to the Children's Courts, the Police Courts, the Assistance Publique, the Buvette, the cells, to a score of grubby little classrooms fitted with the tricolour and a row of inky forms, and to a hundred stuffy cubby-holes crammed from top to floor with *paperasses*. And everywhere is black, is alive, with lawyers, clusters, swarms of lawyers.

"Marie Dumas, Femme Chapet—you are accused of stealing two nickel-plated spoons from the Bazaar de l'Hotel de Ville where you were employed on the second of November of last year. *Qu'avez-vous à répondre?*"

This is *inside*. We are in the X-ième Chambre Correctionnelle, a criminal court.

"I hadn't meant to keep them, Monsieur le Juge, I only——"

"You deny the offence. And furthermore on a subsequent date [in a nimble quaver] you stole from the said *Grand Magasin* an aluminium saucepan valued at 375 francs."

"Monsieur le Juge, I was trying——"

"You persist in your denial. This is not what I read here. Two months——"

"Monsieur le Président——" a lawyer has just hastened to the bar. "I have the honour to represent Madame Chapet. I apologise. I did not hear the call. With your permission, I will now address the court."

"*Ah, bon,*" says the judge.

"I shall be brief and concise." His client has only been married for a short time, they had the good fortune to secure the lease of a room and a kitchen to themselves, their means are but small. . . . The young woman assured him that she had only taken the spoons home from work in order to match them, the same went for the saucepan, she had wanted to try out whether it fitted the new stove . . . At any rate she had meant to pay for them out of her next wage . . . And

Paris: Summary Justice

there is her youth, M. le Président, twenty-two years
old. . . .

The judge behind a tome had been talking to his assessor.
Now he looked up. " Woman Chapet—two months."

" *Affaire* 4——! "

The next accused is a man who has said *salaud* to a policeman.

" I had just parked my motor-bike, he told me to move on,
he wasn't very polite, I was late, I'd just got off work, *j'étais
énervé*——" Reluctantly, " *Je le regrette.*"

The judge hadn't interrupted because he was talking himself.
Now he said, " Fine of 20,000 francs."

No question about means and earnings had been put.

" *Affaire* 5——! "

That man was a grocer who had filled up some empties
with plain tap-water and sold them as a well-known mineral
water.

He said he couldn't tell the difference himself, and anyway
he was not an *épicier de métier*, he was new in the business.

The procureur, who sits in on such cases, asked from his
umpire's chair, " What was your former occupation ? "

" Wine merchant."

He was not represented and didn't seem to take the whole
thing very seriously. He was wrong.

The mineral water company had constituted itself *partie
civile* and sent most able counsel who presently conjured up
a moving picture of the effects on commerce and on public
health if people were allowed to go about selling tap-water
under famous labels. Even the bench is listening.

" Two years with *sursis* and a fine of 250,000 frs."

Sursis is the French version of the deferred sentence. If the
sentence is long and the deferment *sine die*, a convicted man
may find himself on thin ice.

Meanwhile the guards had led in two handcuffed men,
handcuffed to each other. One of them was a negro. Inside
the dock, the chains were taken off.

Here, the dock, *le box*, is only for people who are already

there is her youth, M. le Président, twenty-two years old. . . .

The judge behind a tome had been talking to his assessor. Now he looked up. " Woman Chapet—two months."

" *Affaire* 4——! "

The next accused is a man who has said *salaud* to a policeman.

" I had just parked my motor-bike, he told me to move on, *he* wasn't very polite, I was late, I'd just got off work, *j'étais énervé*——" Reluctantly, " *Je le regrette.*"

The judge hadn't interrupted because he was talking himself. Now he said, " Fine of 20,000 francs."

No question about means and earnings had been put.

" *Affaire* 5——! "

That man was a grocer who had filled up some empties with plain tap-water and sold them as a well-known mineral water.

He said he couldn't tell the difference himself, and anyway he was not an *épicier de métier*, he was new in the business.

The procureur, who sits in on such cases, asked from his umpire's chair, " What was your former occupation ? "

" Wine merchant."

He was not represented and didn't seem to take the whole thing very seriously. He was wrong.

The mineral water company had constituted itself *partie civile* and sent most able counsel who presently conjured up a moving picture of the effects on commerce and on public health if people were allowed to go about selling tap-water under famous labels. Even the bench is listening.

" Two years with *sursis* and a fine of 250,000 frs."

Sursis is the French version of the deferred sentence. If the sentence is long and the deferment *sine die*, a convicted man may find himself on thin ice.

Meanwhile the guards had led in two handcuffed men, handcuffed to each other. One of them was a negro. Inside the dock, the chains were taken off.

Here, the dock, *le box*, is only for people who are already

245

in custody, and they remain inside it while they are giving their evidence. Free people speak from the floor, and sit with their counsel on a little bench behind the bar.

It is still the turn of another man—at liberty—who had lost his temper. This one had kicked a policeman. He has taken a good lawyer.

" What have you got to say ? " says the judge.

He bravely tells his story. He went to the cinema last summer with his wife and child. It was a Sunday afternoon, it was hot, during the intermission he stepped out into the boulevard and had a glass of beer. When he went back, the manager at the door—it was a tiny cinema—refused to let him in without buying another ticket. He protested that his family and ticket stub were inside, the manager was extremely rude ; our man tried to walk past him, the manager called a policeman and asked him to throw this fellow out. The policeman at once laid hands on him. Outraged, he lost his temper. To-day, he is all meek and mealy mouthed apologies.

The kicked policeman gives evidence ; most decently. He says, *il n'y avait pas de mal*, the accused didn't mean any harm, he didn't know what he was doing ; when he realised he calmed down at once and allowed himself to be led off to the station like a lamb.

" You would have done better for yourself," says the judge, " if you'd done as the cinema manager told you. This will come more expensive. 40,000 frs. and costs."

The negro in the dock had been in prison for thirteen days, he is in arrears with alimony to a wife and child. He is described as a musician.

" You tried to evade payment," says the judge.

His lawyer is a woman. She says that the amount was 20.000 frs. and that was a great deal for her client to find in any month. His livelihood consisted of playing in small orchestras and nowadays he often found himself without an engagement.

"He disappeared," said the judge, "he concealed his address."

"He did not conceal it, Monsieur le Président, he did not have one." The judge wants to go on to something else, but she keeps up her voice. "My client has been trying desperately to scrape a living and that meant jumping at any work that offered, often at an hour's notice." He had had engagements recently in the provinces, first near Deauville, and then an offer to stand in for a man who had fallen ill at a winter resort in the Savoie. "People in my client's position, Monsieur le Président, do not keep on their room in Paris when they go off to work elsewhere. A permanent address is a luxury they cannot afford."

"He did not leave his address," said the Procureur.

"Pay, or one year," said the judge.

"Monsieur le Président—how can my client pay from prison? He's already lost one engagement, I implore you! How can he *ever* pay if he is unable to take any engagement at all? *Monsieur le Président*——"

"Case has been judged."

The second man in the dock was a young country lout; stocky, fair, very dirty and rather bemused.

He is charged with an attempt to steal. He has no lawyer. The judge tells him that he has the right to say whether he wishes to be tried as he is today or in a week's time with counsel for the defence.

"Oh, now," he said with a caged animal look at the dock, the guard. "*Pour en finir.*"

"Very well," said the judge. "You were found sitting inside a Renault motor car which you were intending to drive away and steal."

The boy said, "I was tired, I tried the handle, it was open, I got inside to sleep."

"You have four previous convictions for theft," said the judge.

"I swear I didn't mean to steal the car, I only wanted to sleep."

"You were found sitting in the driver's seat," said the judge. " Why ? "

. . . .

"You were found sitting behind the wheel. Why? Why were you sitting behind the wheel ? Why ? "

" But I can't drive."

" These denials will do you no good."

" I can't drive, I swear I can't, I've never driven a car . . . please find out it's true I can't drive——"

" Eight months," said the judge.

The boy looked simply horror-struck, incredulous—the guards bundled him out.

From then on, I spent more time in the Court of Criminal Appeal.

Cases first tried at Assizes may go to the *Cour de Cassation* ; that court either confirms the verdict or it breaks it, which means that the case must go back to the Assizes for a second trial. Cases first tried *en Correctionnelle* go on to the *Cour d'Appel Correctionnelle*. That court sits—after two p.m.— in one of the more ornate chambers of the Palais ; there is a bench of three, an Avocat général is present, and there is counsel for every appellant. The hearings are usually brief, and so quite a number of cases came on and went in the course of a month of afternoons. My notes are but pages of lists (I cannot write while I listen, I often cannot read what I write). I am choosing a page at random.

The Case of the Student who Took Part in a Political
  Demonstration
The Man who lived on Immoral Earnings
The Man who Stole in Métro Stations
Confusion Obligatoire

Paris: Summary Justice

The Case of the Two Women who Said it was a Matrimonial
  Agency
The Czech Valet who Took 500 Dollars from his Master's
  safe
The Young Man who Hid his Face
" Too Late ! "
The Man who was Advised to Desist

The Student who Took Part in a Demonstration was a
university undergraduate and he had marched for something
or other three years before when he was seventeen years old.
(The reason or political colour of the demonstration did not
come out in the hearing, but the judge very likely knew.)
They were headed for a meeting near the Porte d'Orléans
and there was a clash with other demonstrators which was
followed by a clash with the police and a bit of a general
bagarre. People were picked up and he among them.
Unfortunately there was a bicycle chain in his jacket pocket
(found, he maintained, in the road a few minutes earlier and
picked up more or less mechanically in the spirit of the
occasion.) He was appealing from a sentence of the Correctionnelle in 1956.

He sat on a front bench, looking a very thin and serious
young man next to his more voluminous robed counsel, and
he had a clever, lively face.

The presiding judge said testily, " I fail to appreciate the
reason for this appeal, the sentence was only fifteen days
deferred, your client has behaved himself since—he hasn't
had to serve the fifteen days. What does he have to complain
about ? "

This young man, counsel explained, was a philosophy
student of great brilliance, he had passed his *bachot* with extreme
distinction, he was destined for an academic career. . . .
A prison sentence—even never served. . . . surely, M. Le
Président must understand. . . .

The président said he understood that the young man

wanted it off his record. I can see him now, hunching his head, glaring at the young man. " *Vous êtes dressé contre l'autorité,*" he said in that paternal quaver so many of them here affected, " *vous êtes dressé contre l'autorité* ! "

That appeal was dismissed.

The Man who lived on Immoral Earnings hadn't really lived on them at all ; the earnings were his wife's, and some of them had gone towards paying the nursing home he was sent to when he first found out. He was a middle-aged chap, a business manager in a middling way, married, as he believed, honourably ; they had one son, aged eleven, whom the father adored. They were not at all badly off, but the wife had preferred to go out to work ; she had, she told her husband, an excellent evening job as cashier at a restaurant in the Palais Royal. He found out that she was a prostitute through a routine letter from the Préfecture requesting her to come in for the weekly medical visit.

He took it hard. Despair ; disgust. He would have kicked her out had it not been for the boy, the idea of home. He told her flatly that if she did not give it up at once and for good he'd go to the police. She promised. Meanwhile, the business went to pot ; he fell ill and spent some weeks in a nursing home. His wife came to see him and paid one bill.

There was no money in the bank just then, he told the Juge d'instruction, and he hated debts.

When he came out of the nursing home he found that his wife had not reformed. He did not know where to turn. His first thought was to get the boy out of her reach. He had no longer any family of his own. He went to the police. " Monsieur le Commissaire, will you help me ? " He told the story ; they arrested him. He spent three months *en prison préventive.* He was released some months before his trial at the Correctionnelle. There he was sentenced to eighteen months and a largish fine. He had appealed, and so had not yet begun to serve that sentence.

Paris: Summary Justice

He sat composed, almost listless, seeming to pay no attention to the efforts counsel was making on his behalf.

The court decided—with no further comment—that there were mitigating circumstances in this case, and reduced the sentence to six months with *sursis* and quashed the fine.

The Man who Stole in Métro Stations was an Algerian convicted of stealing and trying to steal from slot machines in the underground. He had been caught at it exactly fifteen times. "*Un spécialiste de ce genre de délit*," the président said. The sentence he had appealed from was one of thirty months and *interdit de séjour*, expulsion from the Paris area " Il faut que cet individu soit sorti de la région parisienne " (presumably out of reach of the underground railway network), said the Avocat général, and the sentence was confirmed.

Confusion Obligatoire arose in an argument about a conviction that had been appealed from because of some technical defect, several indictments had been taken or not been taken as one, or something of that kind. The Avocat général got heated and kept saying, " No, no, no, maître, there is no *confusion obligatoire* ! " It was a technical term, of course, but it sounded engaging.

The Case of the Two Women who Said it was a Matrimonial Agency was the expected farce and none too pleasant. They looked frightful. Fairly young, Toulouse-Lautrec and Mesdames Stonyhearts, all smiles and fingernails. They were the manageresses—still are—of a bureau where men could meet young women, and young women could meet men. Aim—marriage. Receipts—one million francs a month. A young woman complained. Correctionnelle decision—three months and a fine of a hundred thousand francs.

The defence was high and mighty. Two hard-working young business-women doing their best, the world being what it is you can lead men and women to a meeting but you cannot make them become engaged. The bureau had advertisements accepted by the most respectable publications, *France-*

France

Dimanche, La Semaine à Paris, Aux Écoutes, The New York Herald Tribune.

The Avocat général did not concur. He read out the *petites annonces,—"une publicité équivoque et tapageuse."*

The defence read a string of clients' depositions, gentle tales of soporific outings, *des soirées correctes,* at the cinema, at restaurants. —Monsieur Untel qui me fut présenté par l'Agence Colombe est un homme très correct—Monsieur Untel est un homme très bien. J'ai eu depuis le plaisir de le faire connaître à Maman. . . .

The bench retired over that one. Outside, the two young women were joined by their lawyer and a man in a very thick, very new, very yellow camel-hair coat and pointed shoes. Seen at close quarters they looked even more terrifying. They all smoked and chattered and appeared quite unconcerned, while I hung about rather tense and worried about that prison sentence.

It was all right. The court changed it to a fine of half a million francs for each.

The Case of the Czech Valet was hopeless in every way. He had stolen the dollars from his American master who had trusted him; he had four previous convictions for theft. The Correctionnelle had sentenced him to four years and relegation to the country of his origin.

There was a background to it. This rather consumptive looking Czech was once a professional football champion of international renown. When Czechoslovakia played France a decade or so ago, this man left his team and sought political asylum; for a brief hour he made front-page news, he was acclaimed as a fine feather in the Free West's cap. Now the yellowed cuttings repose inside the Correctionnelle dossiers. A small accident, pleurisy, advancing age—within a year or two his career on the field was over. To-day, the faithless servant and the jail-bird is still a political refugee. The fact was evident and counsel pleaded it strongly. In vain. The court—stirred by some half-conscious impulse to do *some-*

thing ?—reduced the prison sentence to three years, but upheld the relegation.

The Very Young Man who Hid his Face. I shall not forget him either. He was extremely fair, nordic, with a slight viking look, a viking who had lived a long time indoors. As he sat in that dock and saw and heard, counsel going on, and the judge, about the stolen cheque and whether or not he had meant to cash it, and the investigation and the dates, he suddenly put his face into his hands and began to weep. He wept almost silently but with convulsive violence. I have seen many people cry in the dock. Most women, particularly young women, accused of stealing do ; some people cry out of general misery or fear, because they feel so low and it's the natural thing to do and perhaps it may even help. That young man wept out of pure shame.

The président said stiffly, " *Vous regrettez? Ah, bon.*" It seemed to mollify them. They made a comment : the accused did not appear to be a man of bad intentions ; and they reduced the sentence from six months to four.

" Too late ! " refers again to *obiter* by the Avocat général. In that case the accused had been tried for some theft in the lower court where he had protested innocence and had been sentenced to ten months. On appeal, he admitted guilt. Counsel pleaded that he had only been an accessory in the matter, was a first offender and might well be given a deferred sentence. " *C'est trop tard !* " the Avocat général had cried, " *Je vois le calcul*—confession in return for deferment, '*je te donne l'aveu, tu me donnes le sursis.*' *Trop tard !* "

The man said, " *J'avais peur.*"

Counsel explained—in so many words—that this was not his client's fault, he was a man of small intelligence and he had been pressed [sic] by his counsel in the lower court to admit nothing.

Judgment confirmed, appeal dismissed—*l'affaire a été bien jugée.* . .

France

Not well managed, was the comment of the lawyers in the hall ; lucky not to have had the sentence raised.

The Man who was Advised to Desist had been brought into the dock for the day, from his prison where he was serving a sentence for rape. When his case was called, there was a minute's whispering between him and counsel as a result of which counsel told the court that his client wished to desist from the appeal.

" An excellent idea, that is the best he can do," said the president, with such a full note of sinister congratulation that it left one wondering.

I remember that at this point I fled again for a breath of air. Not that there was much choice, at the Cour d'Assises they were trying an Algerian who had knifed another in a drunken quarrel, downstairs in the Police Courts they were hammering out fines to motorists and their likes in francs instead of sterling and only a very little faster. I went once more to one of the *Chambres Correctionnelles.* They can be told apart by the numbers on the doors ; inside, those tread-mills appear to be one much like the other, the same face, or almost, on the bench, the same crowds and guards, the men clanked in and out of the docks, the lawyers hurtling themselves to and fro. . . .

" Dupont, Jacques—you are charged with behaviour likely to outrage public decency. *Qu'avez-vous a répondre ?* "

" The car was parked—if you can call it so—in a remote countryside in Brittany ; the car, M. le Président, was standing in a field. It was after midnight, on the 13th of July of the year before the last, the Eve of the National Fête, my client and the young lady were driving home after a dance on the coast.

" Monsieur le Président, *la veille d'un Quatorze Juillet— c'était dans l'air—dans la chaleur de l'été* . . .

" It was dark, there was no-one about. No-one saw, no-one could have seen. No-one's morality was affected, no-one would ever have known if the young lady later on had not talked . . .

" Jealousy, gossip, evil tongues . . .

" My client, as you can see, is not a man in his first youth, he is a married man, a family man, a civil servant, a man of position—for eighteen months now, M. le Président, this charge has been hanging over him."

" Four months with *sursis* and a fine of 20,000 frs."

" Legrand, Gaston—you are charged with being drunk in the street. *Qu'avez-vous à repondre ?* "

The defendant is rather a red-nosed fellow, and he has no lawyer.

" I was on the way home from my daughter's First Communion."

One could almost hear the wide-awake London magistrate, *mutatis mutandis*, swooping down : There are no First Communions in January.

" *Quoi*——? *Ah, bon.*" But it makes no difference, it doesn't make any difference at all. " Fine of 2,000 frs and fifteen days deferred."

CPSIA information can be obtained
at www.ICGtesting.com
Printed in the USA
LVOW12s1517280917
550414LV00001B/214/P

9 780571 282685